WHERE'S MY ME

The Religious, Philosophical
Poetry
of John Norris of Bemerton

Edited and published
by
Peter D.E. White

St. Andrew's Church, Bemerton

Typeset by
The National Poetry Foundation
Fareham (0329 822218)
(Reg Charity No 283032)

Printed by
Meon Valley Printers
Bishops Waltham (0489 895460)

To my wife, Madge.

I would like to express my gratitude to the following for the help I have received in preparing this collection of poetry:

Miss N. Aubertin–Potter, Sub–Librarian of the Codrington Library, All Souls College, Oxford.

The Librarian and staff of the Sidmouth Library, Devon.

The Librarian of Exeter Cathedral Library, Devon.

Mr Robert Roberts of Budleigh Salterton for the translation of the memorial plaque.

The Keeper of Western Manuscripts at the Bodleian Library, Oxford, for permission to reproduce the signature of John Norris contained in a manuscript TANNER 41, folio 184.

The Church Wardens and members of Bemerton P.C.C. for permission to use the drawing of the Church.

Mr Michael Hooper B.A., M.A. of Sidmouth for his assistance in reading the proofs.

The cover shows the bust of John Norris that stands in the Codrington Library. This is reproduced by permission of the Warden and fellows of All Souls College, Oxford.

ISBN 1 870556 36 4
£8.50

CONTENTS

***

INTRODUCTION

Many years ago I came across a poem by John Norris called 'A Wish', the content of which agreed entirely with my desire to depart this life accompanied by strains of some beautiful piece of music. At the time, I had no idea who John Norris was or whether he had written any other poetry. This poem was borrowed and not returned, causing me to look for another copy. I soon realised, while making enquiries, that the task would not be a simple one, as there was no collection of his poetry at the present time.

The first poem that I discovered was 'Hymn to Darkness' in the *Metaphysical Poets* by Helen Gardner and the second one, called 'The Retirement' was found in a book on 17th Century minor poets. On learning that John Norris had been the vicar of Bemerton, I went to Salisbury Library, but all they could find was a leaflet of four poems by Norris put together by a gentleman "for his friends" in the 1800's. One of these poems, to my delight, was 'A Wish'.

I then visited the 13th century chapel at South Bemerton, found a plaque on the north wall to the memory of John Norris and saw the old rectory which was his home for twenty years.

My next discovery was some publications of the 1690's by Norris at Exeter Cathedral Library including *Poems and Discourses* of 1684; this brought my collection to 17 poems. I then made contact with the Codrington Library at All Souls College, Oxford and they kindly sent me photocopies of the *Miscellanies* of 1687. I now had 73 poems.

This present collection was put together and corrected from the last edited edition of the *Miscellanies* by the Rev. Alexander B. Grosart in 1871. I trust that it may raise a memorial to John Norris and bring pleasure to poetry lovers everywhere.

Peter White
Sidmouth
Devon

WHO WAS JOHN NORRIS?

John Norris was born on the 2nd January 1657 at Collingbourne–Kingston, Wiltshire, where his father, also John Norris, was the Rector. The family then moved to Aldbourne, in the same county, and it was here that young John spent his early childhood with his two brothers and a sister.

In 1671 John went to Winchester School and the following letter was sent to Exeter College, Oxford, recommending that they should accept him for further education:

> "Having received a very good character of John Norris, a youth in our Schoole as to his proficiency since his coming thither, and the progresse he will likely, if continued there, to make in Learning; I have thought fit to write to you in his behalfe and to desire you to admit him Childe of your Colledge at your next election, if you find him (as I am informed you will) well qualifyed, and very capable of your favour in this particular, to which he is very earnestly recommended by
>
> Your Visitor and
> very loving friend
> George Morley."

John entered Exeter College in 1676 and obtained his Bachelor of Arts degree on the 16th June 1680; in the same year he was appointed a fellow of All Souls College by the Archbishop of Canterbury, William Sancroft. (Incidentally, it was Sancroft with other Anglican bishops who crowded round the dying monarch, Charles the Second, urging him to take the protestant communion: "It is time to speak out," pleaded Sancroft, "for your Majesty is about to appear before a Judge who is no respector of persons.")

John Norris was described by the Warden, Leopold–William Finch, to whom he dedicated his *Miscellanies*, "as a very excellent scholar and one who spoke verses in the Theater with very great Applause, a very good Grecian and philosopher and a young Batchelour of Arts." Other quotations about John Norris are:

> "Having made a good proficiency in classical learning in school, he applied with greater advantage to the academical studies; wherein, not contenting himself with the lesser systems of the sciences usually taught by tutors in the university, he went to the fountain–head and took into his hands the ancient, great masters of philosophy, Plato, Xenophon and Aristotle. Being particularly delighted with the first of these, he studied his works with extraordinary diligence and drank in his notions with eagerness."

He was later known as the "last of the Cambridge Platonists". "John Norris had always the character of an ingenious, sober and industrious man." "A very amiable and pious man with much enthusiasm, a pure and affectionate character."

On the 22nd April 1684 he obtained his Master of Arts degree and in 1687, while still at Oxford, published his most popular book, *A Collection of Miscellanies: consisting of Poems, Essays, Discourses and Letters, occasionally written.* It went through nine editions. In his dedication to the Warden he writes "To you therefore I humbly present this

Collection of Miscellanies for the entertainment of your leisure hours, which were composed at some of mine."

John Norris was ordained in 1684 and left Oxford in 1689 to take up a living at Newton St. Loe in Somerset. He married in the same year and Elizabeth, his wife, bore him four children, John, Edward, Elizabeth and Thomas.

In 1692 John Norris became the Rector of Bemerton, near Salisbury. (Now St. Andrew's Church or George Herbert's Chapel.) Here he lived a quiet and placid life as a country parson and thinker. With his strong memory and wide reading he was able to answer questions sent in to the *Athenian Gazette*, to which he made a useful contribution. Although he produced 23 publications, many of them popular and going through several editions, they brought him little profit. His income in 1707 was £70 p.a. and he said "the world ran strait and hard" with him.

He was rather an isolated figure among the poets of the 1680's. Most of his poetry, which is full of "small felicities and conceits" was probably written while he was a fellow of All Souls College. The theme of his non-religious poetry is of retirement, of contentment with little, the blessing of obscurity and the superiority of meditation and learning over riches and mundane glory. Lady Chudleigh, a friend, wrote of Norris: "He was a little man with a pale complexion but he also had plenty of kindness and good humour in his face, combined with an extraordinary modesty and an air of considerable humility. There seems to be a reservedness in his temper, but when you know him you find it is only the result of thoughtfulness. In a word he is a man whose conversation is very agreeable while at the same time being instructive."

In 1704 while working on his *Theory of the Ideal World* he writes of losing the sight of one eye: "... so many thoughtful and solitary hours, so many nightly lamps and lucubrations, have these studies cost me, that indeed my poor eyes, (what with age and what with assiduous poring,) have the one departed this world and the other almost worn itself out with incessant grief for the loss of its fellow..."

When writing his treatise on *Christian Prudence* in 1710 he mentions his failing health: "And I could wish that some other more able hand would go on with the rest, it being for one of my little health and less abilities too great an undertaking." This was to be his last work. After serving his parish for 20 years he died and was buried at Bemerton on the 5th February 1711, aged only 54 years. The probable cause of his premature demise was given as "having exhausted his strength by intense application and long habits of severe reasoning." R.A. Willmott, 1841.

P.W.

Then as for glory which comes after Fate,
    All that can then of me be said
I value least of all, it comes too late,
    'Tis like th'embalming of the senseless dead.
Others with pleasure, what me labour cost
    May read, and praise, but to me all is lost.
Just as the Sun no joy does find
    In that his light which cheers mankind.

Or grant 'twou'd pleasure bring to know that I
    After my death live still in Fame,
Those that admire me too must shortly dye,
    And then where's my Memorial, where my name?
My Fame tho' longer-lived, yet once shall have
    Like me its Death, its Funeral, its Grave.
This only difference will remain,
    I shall, that never rise again.

From 'The Indifferency' by John Norris.

"To you therefore I humbly present this Collection of Miscellanies for the entertainment of your leisure hours, which were composed at some of mine."

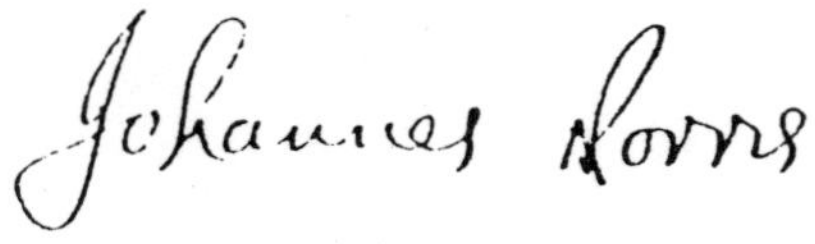

THE PASSION OF OUR BLESSED SAVIOUR, REPRESENTED IN A PINDARIQUE ODE

Say bold licentious[1] Muse,
What noble subject wilt thou chuse;
Of what great hero, of what mighty thing,
Wilt thou in boundless numbers sing?
Sing the unfathom'd depths of Love,
– For who the wonders done by Love can tell,
By Love which is it self all miracle? –
Here in vast endless circles may'st thou rove;
And like the travelling planet of the day
In an orb unbounded stray.
Sing the great miracle of Love divine,
Great be thy genius, sparkling every line,
Love's greatest mystery rehearse:
Greater than that,
Which on the teeming chaos brooding sate,
And hatch'd with kindly heat the Universe.
How God in mercy chose to bleed, and dye,
To rescue man from misery:
Man, not His creature only, but His enemy.

Lo, in Gethsemane, I see Him prostrate lye,
Press'd with the weight of His great agony.
The common sluces of the eyes
To vent His mighty Passion won't suffice,
His tortured body weeps all–o're,
And out of every pore
Buds forth a gem of purple gore.
How strange the power of Afflication's rod
When in the hand of an incensèd God!

[1] = unrestrained

Like the commanding wand
In Moses's hand,[1]
It works a miracle, and turns the flood
Of tears into a sea of blood.
See with what pomp Sorrow does now appear!
How proud she is of being seated here!
She never wore
So rich a dye before.
Long was He willing to decline
Th' encounter of the wrath divine.
Thrice He sent for His release
Pathetick embassies of peace:
At length, His courage overcame His doubt,
Resolv'd He was, and so the bloody flag hung out.[2]

And now the tragic scene's display'd,
Where drawn in full battalia are laid
Before His eyes,
That numerous host of miseries
He must withstand, that map of woe
Which He must undergo.
That heavy wine-press which must by Him be trod,
The whole artillery of God.
He saw that face, whose very sight
Chears angels with its beatific light,
Contracted now into a dreadful frown,
All cloath'd with thunder, big with death
And showers of hot burning wrath,
Which shortly must be pourèd down.
He saw a black and dismal scroll,
Of sins past, present, and to come,
With their intolerable doom

[1] = Exodus 7:19
[2] = the flag of surrender to the will of God. Matthew 26:39

Which would the more oppress His spotless soul;
As th' elements are weighty proved,
When from their native station they'r removed.
He saw the foul ingratitude of those,
Who would the labours of His love oppose;
And reap no benefit by all His agonies.
He saw all this,
And as He saw, to waver He began,
And almost to repent of His great love for man.

When lo, a heavenly form all bright and fair,
Swifter than thought, shot through th' enlighten'd air.
He who sat next th' imperial throne,
And read the counsels of the Great Three-One,
Who in eternity's mysterious glass,
Saw both what was, what is, and what must come to pass;
He came with reverence profound,
And rais'd his prostrate Maker from the ground;
Wiped off the bloody sweat
With which His face and garments too were wet:
And comforted His dark benighted mind,
With sovereign cordials of light refin'd.
This done, in soft addresses he began
To fortifie His kind designs for man:
Unseal'd to Him the Book of God's decree,
And shew'd Him what must be:
Alleg'd the truth of prophesies,
Types, figures, and mysteries;
How needful it was to supply,
With humane race, the ruins of the sky.
How this would bring
To the celestial quire;

And how withall, it would inspire
New matter for the praise of the great King.
How He should see the travail of His soul, and bless
Those sufferings, which had so good success.
How great the triumphs of His victory,
How glorious His ascent would be,
What weighty bliss in Heaven He should obtain
By a few hours of pain;
Where to eternal ages He should reign.
He spake: confirm'd in mind the champion stood;
A spirit divine
Through the thick veil of flesh did shine:
All–over powerful He was, all–over good.
Pleas'd with his successful flight,
The officious[1] angel posts away
To the bright regions of eternal day;
Departing in a track of light.
In haste for news, the heavenly people ran,
And joy'd to hear the hopeful state of man.

And now that strange prodigious hour,
When God must subject be to humane[2] power;
That hour is come,
Th' unerring clock of Fate has struck
'Twas heard below down to Hell's lowest room,
And straight th' infernal powers th' appointed signal took.
Open the scene, my Muse, and see
Wonders of impudence and villany;
How wicked mercenary hands,
Dare to invade Him whom they should adore;
With swords and staves, encompass'd round He stands,
Who knew no other guards but those of Heaven before.

[1] = complaisant
[2] = human

Once with His powerful breath, He did repell
The rude assaults of Hell.
A ray of His divinity
Shot forth with that bold answer, *'I am He'*:
They reel and stagger, and fall to the ground;[1]
For God was in the sound.
The Voice of God was once again,
Walking in the Garden, heard:[2]
And once again, was by the guilty hearers fear'd:
Trembling seiz'd every joint, and chilness every vein.
This little Victory He won,
Shew'd what He could have done.
But He to whom as chief was given,
The whole militia of Heaven,
That mighty He,
Declines all guards for His defence,
But that of His inseparable innocence;
And quietly gives up His liberty.
He's seiz'd on by the military bands,
With cords they bind His sacred hands:
But ah! how weak, what nothings would they prove,
Were He not held by stronger ones of Love.

Once more, my weary'd Muse, thy pinions try,
And reach the top of Calvary.
A steep ascent: but most to Him Who bore
The burthen of a cross this way before.
– The cross ascends, there's something in it sure
That moral is and mystical;
No heights of Fortune are from thee secure,
Afflictions sometimes climb as well as fall –
Here breathe a while, and view

[1] = John 18:6
[2] = Genesis 3:8

The dolefull'st picture Sorrow ever drew:
The Lord of Life, Heaven's darling Son,
The great, th' Almighty One,
With out-stretch'd arms, nail'd to a cursèd tree,
Crown'd with sharp thorns, cover'd with infamy:
He Who before
So many miracles had done,
The lives of others to restore,
Does with a greater, lose His Own.
Full three long hours His tender body did sustain,
Most exquisite and poignant pain.
So long the sympathising sun his light withdrew,
And wonder'd how the stars their dying Lord could view.

This strange defect of light,
Does all the sages in Astronomy affright,
With fears of an eternal night.
Th' intelligences in their courses stray,
And travellers below mistake their way;
Wond'ring to be benighted in the midst of day.
Each mind is seiz'd with horror and despair,
And more o'erspread with darkness than the air.
Fear on, 'tis wondrous all, and new;
'Tis what past ages never knew.
Fear on, but yet you'll find,
The great eclipse is still behind.
The lustre of the Face divine,
Does on the mighty Sufferer no longer shine.
God hides His glories from His sight,
With a thick skreen made of Hell's grossest night.
Close-wrought it was, and solid, all
Compacted and substantial;
Impenetrable to the beatifick light.

Without complaint, He bore
The tortures He endur'd before;
But now, no longer able to contain,
Under the great hyperbole of pain,
He mourns, and with a strong pathetic cry,
Laments the sad destruction of the deity.
Here stop, my Muse, stop and admire,
The breather of all life does now expire:
His milder Father summons him away;
His breath obediently He does resign:
Angels to Paradise His soul convey;
And calm the relicts of His grief with hymns divine.

"This ode is after the Pindarique way; which is the highest and most magnificent kind of writing in verse; and consequently fit only for great and noble subjects ... the nature of which is to be loose and free; and not to keep one settled pace: but sometimes like a gentle stream, to glide along peaceably within its own channel; and sometimes, like an impetuous torrent, to roll on extravagantly, and carry all before it." J.N.

A HYMN UPON THE TRANSFIGURATION

Hail, King of Glory, clad in robes of light,
Out-shining all we here call bright:
Hail Light's divinest galaxy,
Hail express image of the deity.[1]
Could now thy amorous Spouse Thy beauties view,

[1] = Hebrews 1:3

How would her wounds all bleed anew!
Lovely Thou art all o're and bright,
Thou Israel's glory, and Thou Gentile's light.

But whence this brightness, whence this suddain day?
Who did Thee thus with light array?
Did thy divinity dispence
T' its consort a more liberal influence?
Or did some curious angel's chymick art[1]
The spirits of purest light impart,
Drawn from the native spring of Day,
And wrought into an organizèd ray?

How e're 'twas done, 'tis glorious and divine,
Thou dost with radiant wonders shine,
The sun with his bright company,
Are all gross meteors if compar'd to Thee.
Thou art the fountain whence their light does flow,
But to Thy will Thine own dost owe.
For – as at first – Thou didst but say,
"Let there be light," and straight sprang forth this wondrous day.

Let now the Eastern princes come and bring
Their tributary offering.
There needs no star to guide their flight,
They'll find Thee now, great King, by Thine Own light.
And thou, my soul, adore, love, and admire,
And follow this bright guide of fire.
Do thou thy hymns and praises bring
Whil'st angels with veil'd faces, anthems sing.

[1] = the art of the chemist

THE PARTING

Depart! The sentence of the damn'd I hear;
Compendious[1] grief, and black despair.
I now believe the Schools with ease,
– Tho once a happy infidel –
That should the sense no torment sieze,
Yet pain of loss alone would make a Hell.

Take all, since me of this, you Gods, deprive,
'Tis hardly worth while to live.
Nought in exchange can grateful prove,
No second friendship can be found
To match my mourning widow'd love;
Eden is lost, the rest's but common ground.

Why are the greatest blessings sent in vain,
Which must be lost with greater pain?
Or why do we fondly admire
The greatest good which life can boast?
When fate will have the bliss expire:
Like life, with painful agonies 'tis lost.

How fading are the joys we dote upon,
Like apparitions seen and gone:
But those which soonest take their flight,
Are the most exquisite and strong.
Like angels' visits, short and bright;
Mortality's too weak to bear them long.

[1] = full but concise

No pleasure certainly is so divine
As when two souls in love combine:
He has the substance of all bliss,
To whom a vertuous friend is given:
So sweet harmonious friendship is
Add but eternity, you'll make it Heaven.

The minutes in your conversation spent
Were festivals of true content.
Here, here, an ark of pleasing rest,
My soul had found that restless dove,
My present state methought was best,
I envy'd none below, scarce those above.

But now the better part of me is gone,
My sun is set, my turtle flown.[1]
Tho here and there of lesser bliss
Some twinkling stars give feeble light,
Still there a mournful darkness is,
They shine but just enough to shew 'tis night.

Fatal divorce! What have I done amiss,
To bear such misery as this?
The world yields now no real good,
All happiness is now become
But painted and deluding food:
As meer a fiction as Elysium.

[1] = Song of Solomon 2:12

Well then, since nothing else can please my taste,
I'll ruminate on pleasures past.
So when with glorious visions blest,
The waking hermit finds no theme
That's grateful to his thoughtful breast,
He sweetly recollects his pleasing dream.

TO A LADY, SUPPOSED TO ASK, WHAT LIFE WAS?

'Tis not because I breathe and eat,
'Tis not because a vigorous heat
Drives round my blood, and does impart
Motion to my pulse and heart:
'Tis not such proofs as these can give
Any assurance that I live:
No, no, to live is to enjoy;
What marrs our bliss does life destroy:
The days which pass without content,
Are not liv'd properly, but spent.
Who says the damn'd in Hell do live?
That word we to the blessèd give:
The sum of all whose happiness
We by the name of life express.
Well then, if this account be true,
To live is still to live with you.[1]

[1] = written while still a single man

THE THIRD CHAPTER OF JOB PARAPHRASED

Curs'd, ever curs'd be that unhappy day
When first the sun's unwelcom ray
I saw with trembling eyes, being newly come
From the dark prison of the womb.
When first to me my vital breath was lent,
That breath which now must all in sighs be spent.

Let not the sun his chearing beams display
Upon that wretched, wretched day;
But mourn in sables, and all over shroud
His glories in a sullen cloud.
Let light to upper regions be confin'd,
And all below as black as is my mind.

Curs'd be the night which first began to lay
The ground–work of this house of clay:
Let it not have the honour to appear
In the retinue of the year.
Let all the days shun its society,
Hate, curse, abandon it as much as I.

Let Melancholy call that night her own,
Then let her sigh, then let her groan:
A general grief throughout all Nature spread,
With folded arms, and drooping head.
All harps be still, or tun'd to such a strain
As fiends might hear, and yet not ease their pain.

Let neither moon nor stars, with borrow'd light,
Checquer the blackness of that night:
But let a pure unquestion'd darkness rear
Her sooty wings all o're the air;
Such as once on th' abyss of chaos lay,
Not to be pierc'd by stars, scarce by the edge of Day.

Why was there then, ah, why a passage free
At once for life and misery?
Why did I not uncloister'd from the womb
Take my next lodging in a tomb?
Why with such cruel tenderness and care
Was I nurs'd up to sorrow and despair?

For now in sweet repose might I have lain
Secure from any grief or pain:
Untouch'd with care, my bed I should have made
In death's cool and refreshing shade.
I should have slept now in a happy place,
All calm and silent as the empty space.

There where great emperours their heads lay down,
Tir'd with the burthen of a crown.
There where the mighty, popular and great,
Are happy in a dear retreat;
Enjoy that solid peace which here in vain,
In grotts and shady walks they sought t' obtain.

None of Hell's agents can or dare molest
This awful sanctuary of rest.
No prisoner's sighs, no groanings of the slave,
Disturb the quiet of the grave.
From toil and labour here they ever cease,
And keep a sabbath of sweet rest and peace.

Why then does Heaven on mortals life bestow
When 'tis thus overtax'd with woe?
Why am I forc'd to live against my will,
When all the good is lost in ill?
My sighs flow thick, my groans sound from afar,
Like falling waters to the traveller.

SERAPHIC LOVE

'Tis true, frail Beauty, I did once resign
To thy imperious charms this heart of mine.
There didst thou undisturb'd thy scepter sway,
And I methought was pleas'd t'obey.
Thou seem'st so lovely, so divine,
With such sweet graces didst thou shine,
Thou entertain'st my amorous sense,
With such harmonious excellence,
That, credulous and silly I,
With vain, with impious idolatory,
Ador'd that star which was to lead me to the Deity.

But now, thou soft enchantress of the mind,
Farewel! a change, a mighty change I find;
The empire of my heart thou must resign,
For I can be no longer thine.
A nobler, a diviner guest,
Has took possession of my breast;
He has, and must engross it all,
And yet the room is still too small.
In vain you tempt my heart to rove,
A fairer object now my soul does move,
It must be all devotion, what before was love.

Through Contemplation's optics I have seen
Him who is "fairer than the sons of men":[1]
The source of good, the light archetypall,
Beauty in the original.
"The fairest of ten thousand" He
Proportion all and harmony.
All mortal beauty's but a ray
Of His bright ever–shining day;
A little feeble twinkling star,
Which now the sun's in place must disappear;
There is but One that's good, there is but One that's fair.

To thee, Thou only fair, my soul aspires
With holy breathings, languishing desires.
To Thee m' inamoured, panting heart does move,
By efforts of ecstatic love.
How do Thy glorious streams of light
Refresh my intellectual sight!
Tho broken, and strain'd through a skreen
Of envious flesh that stands between!

[1] = Psalm 45:2

When shall m' imprison'd soul be free,
That she Thy native uncorrected light may see,
And gaze upon Thy beatifick face to all eternity?

THE RETIREMENT

Well, I have thought on't, and I find
This busie world is nonsense all;
I here despair to please my mind,
Her sweetest honey is so mixt with gall.
Come then, I'll try how 'tis to be alone,
Live to my self a while, and be my own.

Iv'e try'd, and bless the happy change;
So happy, I could almost vow
Never from this retreat to range,
For sure I ne'er can be so blest as now.
From all th' alloys of bliss I here am free,
I pity others, and none envy me.

Here in this shady lonely grove,
I sweetly think my hours away,
Neither with business vex'd, nor love,
Which in the world bear such tyrannick sway:
No tumults can my close apartment find,
Calm as those seats above, which know no storm nor wind.

Let plots and news embroil the State,
Pray what's that to my books and me?
Whatever be the kingdom's fate,
Here I am sure t' enjoy a monarchy.
Lord of my self, accountable to none,
Like the first man in Paradise, alone.

While the ambitious vainly sue,
And of the partial stars complain,
I stand upon the shore and view
The mighty labours of the distant main,
I'm flush'd with silent joy, and smile to see
The shafts of Fortune still drop short of me.

Th' uneasy pageantry of State,
And all the plagues to thought and sense
Are far remov'd; I'm plac'd by Fate
Out of the road of all impertinence.
Thus, tho my fleeting life runs swiftly on,
'Twill not be short, because 'tis all my own.

THE INFIDEL

Farewel fruition[1], thou grand cruel cheat
Which first our hopes does raise and then defeat.
Farewel thou midwife to abortive bliss,
Thou mystery of fallacies.
Distance presents the object fair,

[1] = pleasure from possessions

With charming features and a graceful air,
But when we come to seize th' inviting prey,
Like a shy ghost, it vanishes away.

So to th' unthinking boy the distant sky
Seems on some mountain's surface to rely;
He with ambitious haste climbs the ascent,
Curious to touch the firmament:
But when with an unweary'd pace
Arriv'd he is at the long–wish'd–for place,
With sighs the sad defeat he does deplore,
His heaven is still as distant as before.

And yet 'twas long e're I could throughly see
This grand impostor's frequent treachery.
Tho often fool'd, yet I should still dream on
Of pleasure in reversion.
Tho still he did my hopes deceive,
His fair pretensions I would still believe.
Such was my charity, that tho I knew
And found him false, yet I would think him true.

But now he shall no more with shews deceive,
I will no more enjoy, no more believe.
Th' unwary jugler has so often shewn
His fallacies, that now they'r known,
Shall I trust on? the cheat is plain,
I will not be impos'd upon again.
I'll view the bright appearance from afar,
But never try to catch the falling star.

ON A MUSICIAN SUPPOSED TO BE MAD WITH MUSICK

Poor dull mistake of low mortality,
To call that madness which is ecstacy.
'Tis no disorder of the brain,
His soul is only set t' an higher strain.
Out–soar he does the sphere of common sense,
Rais'd to diviner excellence;
But when at highest pitch, his soul out–flies,
Not reason's bounds, but those of vulgar eyes.

So when the mystick Sibyl's[1] sacred breast
Was with divine infusions possest,
'Twas rage and madness thought to be,
Which was all oracle and mystery.
And so the soul that's shortly to commence
A spirit free from dregs of sense,
Is thought to rave, when she discourses high,
And breathes the lofty strains of immortality.

Musick, thou generous ferment of the soul,
Thou universal cement of the whole;
Thou spring of passion, that dost inspire
Religious ardours, and poetic fire,
Who'd think that madness should b' ascribed to thee,
That mighty discord to thy harmony?
But 'twas such ignorance that call'd the gift divine
Of various tongues, rage, and th' effects of wine.[2]

[1] = one of several women of the ancient world who prophesied under the inspiration of some god
[2] = Acts 2:4–18

But thou, seraphick soul, do thou advance
In thy sweet ecstacy, thy pleasing trance:
Let thy brisk passions mount still higher,
Till they join to the element of fire.
Soar higher yet, till thou shalt calmly hear
The musick of a well–tun'd sphere:
Then on the lumpish mass look down, and thou shalt know
The madness of the world, for groveling still below.

THE CONSOLATION

I grant 'tis bad, but there is some relief
In the society of Grief.
'Tis sweet to him that mourns, to see
A whole house clad in Sorrow's livery.
Grief in communion does remiss appear,
Like harsher sounds in consort,[1] which less grate the ear.

Men would not curse the stars did they dispense
In common their ill influence.
Let none be rich, and poverty
Would not be thought so great a misery.
Our discontent is from comparison;
Were better states unseen, each man would like his own.

Should partial seas wreck my poor ship alone,
I might with cause my fate bemoan.
But since before I sink, I see

[1] = concert

A numerous fleet of ships descend with me,
Why don't I with content my breath resign?
I will, and in the greater ruine bury mine.

THE CHOICE

No, I shan't envy him, who'er he be,
That stands upon the battlements of state;
Stand there who will for me,
I'd rather be secure than great.
Of being so high the pleasure is but small,
But long the ruin, if I chance to fall.

Let me in some sweet shade serenely lye,
Happy in leisure and obscurity;
Whilst others place their joys
In popularity and noise.
Let my soft minutes glide obscurely on,
Like subterraneous streams, unheard, unknown.

Thus when my days are all in silence past
A good plain country-man I'll dye at last.
Death cannot chuse but be
To him a mighty misery,
Who to the world was popularly known,
And dies a stranger to himself alone.

THE MEDITATION

It must be done – my soul – but 'tis a strange,
A dismal and mysterious change,
When thou shalt leave this tenement of clay,
And to an unknown somewhere wing away;
When Time shall be Eternity, and thou
Shalt be thou know'st not what, and live thou know'st not how.

Amazing state! No wonder that we dread
To think of death, or view the dead.
Thou'rt all wrapt up in clouds, as if to thee
Our very knowledge had antipathy.
Death could not a more sad retinue find,
Sickness and Pain before, and Darkness all behind.

Some courteous ghost, tell this great secrecy,
What 'tis you are, and we must be.
You warn us of approaching death, and why
May we not know from you what 'tis to dye?
But you, having shot the gulph, delight to see
Succeeding souls plunge in with like uncertainty.

When life's close knot by writ from Destiny,
Disease shall cut, or age unty;
When after some delays, some dying strife,
The soul stands shivering on the ridge of life;
With what a dreadful curiosity
Does she launch out into the sea of vast Eternity!

So when the spacious globe was delug'd o'er,
And lower holds could save no more,
On th' utmost bough th' astonished sinners stood,
And view'd th' advances of th' encrouching flood.
O'er topp'd at length by th' element's encrease,
With horror they resign'd to the untry'd abyss.

THE IRRECONCILABLE

I little thought – my Damon – once, that you
Could prove, and what is more, to me, untrue.
Can I forget such treachery and live?
Mercy it self would not this crime forgive.
Heaven's gates refuse to let apostates in,
No, that's the great unpardonable sin.

Did you not vow by all the powers above,
That you could none but dear Orinda love?
Did you not swear by all that is divine,
That you would only be and ever mine?
You did, and yet you live securely too,
And think that Heaven's false as well as you.

Believe me, love's a thing much too divine
Thus to be ap'd, and made a mere design.
'Tis no less a crime than treason here to feign,
'Tis counterfeiting of a royal coin.
But ah! Hypocrisy's no where so common grown
As in most sacred things, Love and Religion.

Go seek new conquests, go, you have my leave,
You shall not grieve her whom you could deceive.
I don't lament, but pity what you do,
Nor take that love as lost, which ne'r was true.
The way that's left you to befriend my fate,
Is now to prove more constant in your hate.

THE ADVICE

What's forming in the womb of Fate
Why art thou so concern'd to know?
Dost think 'twou'd be advantage to thy state?
But wiser Heaven does not think it so.
With thy content thou wouldst this knowledge buy,
No part of life thou'dst pleasant find
For dread of what thou see'st behind,
Thou would'st but tast of the inlightning fruit and dye.

Well then, has Heaven events to come
Hid with the blackest veil of Night;
But still in vain if we forestall our doom,
And with prophetick fears our selves affright:
Grand folly! whether thus 'twill be or no
We know not, and yet silly man
Secures his evils what he can,
And stabs himself with grief, lest Fate should miss the blow.

Be wise, and let it be thy care
To manage well the present hour;
Call home thy ranging thoughts and fix them here.
This only mind, this only's in thy power.
The rest no settled, steddy course maintain,
Like rivers, which now gently slide
Within their bounds, now with full tide
O'erflow, whom houses, cattle, trees resist in vain.

'Tis he that's happy, he alone
Lives free and pleasant that can say
With every period of the setting sun,
I've lived, and run my race, like him to day.
To morrow let the angry heavens frown,
Or smile with influence more kind,
On chance depends what's yet behind,
But sure what I have seiz'd already's all my own.

Fortune who no diversion knows
Like Disappointment, laughs to see
How variously she can her gifts transpose,
Sometimes to one, sometimes t'another free.
Be sure to enjoy her while she's pleas'd to stay.
But if for flight she does prepare,
Don't you at parting drop a tear,
But hold your virtue fast, for that alone you may.

TO HIMSELF

Not yet convinc'd? why wilt thou still pursue
Through nature's field delusive bliss?
'Tis false, or else too fugative if true;
Thou may'st assoon thy shadow overtake as this.
The gaudy light still dances in thy eye;
Thou hot and eager in the chase
Art drawn through many a thorny rugged place,
Still labouring and sighing, but can'st ne'er come nigh.

Give o're my soul, give o're, not strive again
This treacherous chymic gold to find.
Tell me, why shouldst thou fancy there remain
Days yet to come more sweet, than those thou'st left behind.
A wiser chymist far than thou, t'obtain
This jewel all his treasures spent,
But yet he fail'd in's grand experiment,
And all he gain'd was this, to know that all was vain.[1]

Forbear, and at another's cost be wise,
Nor longer this coy mistress woo.
He's mad that runs where none can win the prize,
Why should'st thou lose thy mistress, and thy labour too?
Heaven does but sport with our simplicity
By laying jewels in our way,
For when we stoop to seize the glittering prey,
They'r snatcht away again, and baulk our greedy eye.

[1] = Ecclesiastes 12:8

'Tis so, the choicest good this world can give
Will never stand fruition's test.
This all by experience find, yet few believe,
And in the midst of cheats hope they shall once be blest.
Strange magick this. So witches tho they find
No comfort from their airy meat,
Forget at next cabal their slender treat,
And greedily again fall to their feast of wind.

But thou my soul thy strong conviction shew,
And never reach at bliss again.
Our best good here is Nature's bounds to know,
And those attempts to spare, which else would be in vain.
Here then contain thy self, nor higher good
In this inchanted place pursue.
And pity those short–sighted souls that do;
The world is best enjoy'd, when 'tis best understood.

THE REFUSAL

Think not to court me from my dear retreat,
No I protest 'tis all in vain.
My stars did never mean I should be great,
And I the very thought disdain.
Or, if they did, their will I'll disobey,
And in my little orb remain as fix'd as they.

Honour, that idol which the most adore,
Receives no homage from my knee.
Content in privacy, I value more
Than all uneasie dignity.
How should that empty thing deserve my care,
Which Virtue does not need, and Vice can never bear?

Shall I change solid and unenvy'd joys
Of a serene, tho humble state,
For splendid trouble, pomp and senseless noise?
This I despise as well as hate.
Poor gain of that condition, which will be
Envy'd by others, and as much dislik'd by me.

HYMN TO DARKNESS

Hail thou most sacred venerable thing!
What Muse is worthy thee to sing?
Thee, from whose pregnant universal womb
All things, even Light thy rival, first did come.
What dares he not attempt that sings of thee
Thou first and greatest mystery?
Who can the secrets of thy essence tell?
Thou like the light of God art inaccessible.

Before great Love this monument did raise,
This ample theatre of praise.
Before the folding circles of the sky

Were tun'd by Him who is all harmony.
Before the morning stars their hymn began,
Before the councel held for man.
Before the birth of either Time or Place,
Thou reign'st unquestion'd monarch in the empty space.

Thy native lot thou didst to Light resign,
But still half of the globe is thine.
Here with a quiet, and yet aweful hand,
Like the best emperours thou dost command.
To thee the stars above their brightness owe,
And mortals their repose below.
To thy protection Fear and Sorrow flee,
And those that weary are of light, find rest in thee.

Tho light and glory be th' Almighty's throne,
Darkness is His pavilion.[1]
From that His radiant beauty, but from thee
He has His terror and His majesty.
Thus when He first proclaim'd His sacred Law,
And would His rebel subjects awe.
Like princes on some great solemnity,
H'appear'd in's robes of State, and clad Himself with thee.

The blest above do thy sweet umbrage[2] prize,
When cloy'd[3] with light, they veil their eyes.
The vision of the Deity is made
More sweet and beatifick by thy shade.
But we poor tenants of this orb below

[1] = Psalm 18:11
[2] = shadow
[3] = sickened with excess

Don't here thy excellencies know,
Till Death our understandings does improve,
And then our wiser ghosts thy silent night–walks love.

But thee I now admire, thee would I chuse
For my religion, or my Muse.
'Tis hard to tell whether thy reverend shade
Has more good votaries or poets made,
From thy dark caves were inspirations given,
And from thick groves went vows to Heaven.
Hail then thou Muse's and Devotion's spring,
'Tis just we should adore, 'tis just we should thee sing.

THE INVITATION

Come my beloved let us go forth into the field, let us lodge in the villages. (Cantic. vii, 11)

Come thou divinest object of my love,
This noisy region don't with us agree;
Come let us hence remove,
I cannot here enjoy my self or thee.
Here Vice and Folly keep their court,
Hither their chiefest favourites resort,
Debauchery has here her royal chair,
This is her great metropolis,
What e'er we see or hear contagion is;
Their manners are polluted like the air.
From both unwholsom vapours rise
And blacken with ungrateful steams the neighbouring skies.

Come we'll e'n to our country-seat repair,
The native home of Innocence and Love.
There we'll draw purer air,
And pity monarchs, sitting in our grove,
Here Virtue has her safe retreat,
Abandon'd by the many and the great.
Content does here her peaceful scepter sway;
Here Faithfulness and Friendship dwell,
And Modesty has here her humble cell:
Come my Beloved, come, and let's away.
Be thou my angel good and kind,
And I'll n'er look at Sodom which we leave behind.

In fields and flow'ry meadows, woods and groves,
The first and best delights of humane kind,
There we'll enjoy our loves
All free, and only to ourselves confin'd.
Here shall my eyes be fixt on thee,
Till every passion be an extasie.
Each hour to thee shall be canonical;
The sweets of Nature shall not stay
My soul, but only shew to thee the way;
To thee! Thou beauty's great original.
Come my Beloved, let's go prove
These sweet advantages of peace, content, and love.

SITTING IN AN ARBOUR

Thus ye good powers, thus let me ever be
Serene, retir'd, from love and business free;
The rest of your great world I here resign
To the contentions of the great;
I only ask that this retreat,
This little tenement be mine.
All my ambition's to this point confin'd;
Others inlarge their fortunes, I my mind.

How calm, how happy, how serene am I!
How satisfy'd with my own company.
To few things foreign my content I owe;
But in myself have almost all
Which I dare good or pleasing call,
Or – what's as well – I fancy so.
Thus I affect an independent state,
And – as a creature can – in self I terminate.

Pleas'd with a various scene of thought I lie,
Whil'st an obliging stream slides gently by
Silent and deep as is the bliss I chuse;
All round the little wingèd quire,
Pathetic, tender thoughts inspire,
And with their strains provoke my Muse.
With ease the inspiration I obey,
And sing as unconcern'd, and as well pleas'd as they.

If ought below deserve the name of bliss,
It must – whate'er the great ones think – be this.
So once the travelling patriarch doubly blest
With dreams divine from Heaven sent,
And his own heaven of content,
On's rocky pillow took his rest,
Angels stood smiling by and said, were we our bliss
To change, it should be for a state like his.

'Tis strange so cheap, and yet so great a good
Should by so very few be understood.
That bliss which others seek with toil and sweat
For which they prodigally wast
Their treasures, and yet miss at last,
Here I have at an easie rate.
So those that costly physick use in vain,
Sometimes by cheap receipts their health obtain.

THE COMPLAINT

Well 'tis a dull perpetual round
Which here we silly mortals tread;
Here's nought I'll swear worth living to be found,
I wonder how 'tis with the dead.
Better I hope, or else ye powers divine
Unmake me, I my mortality resign.

Still to be vex'd by joys delay'd
Or by fruition to be cloy'd?
Still to be wearied in a fruitless chase,
Yet still to run, and lose the race?
Still our departed pleasures to lament
Which yet when present give us no content?

Is this the thing we so extol,
For which we would prolong our breath?
Do we for this, long life a blessing call
And tremble at the name of Death?
Sots that we are to think by that we gain
Which is as well retain'd as lost with pain.

Is it for this that we adore
Physicians, and their art implore?
Do we bless Nature's liberal supply
Of helps against mortality?
Sure 'tis but vain the tree of life to boast,
When Paradise, wherein it grew, is lost.

Ye powers, why did you man create
With such insatiable desire?
If you'd endow him with no more estate
You should have made him less aspire.
But now our appetites you vex and cheat
With real hunger, and phantastic meat.

A PASTORAL UPON THE BLESSED VIRGIN, GONE FROM NAZARETH TO VISIT ELIZABETH

Wherein the sadness of the country Nazareth is described during the absence of the Virgin.

Translated out of Rapin.[1]
The speakers are *Asor, Alphæus* and *Zebede.*

Asor.

And why Alphæus, in this sweet shade dost thou
Make songs, which are not seasonable now,
Since we of fair Parthenia are bereft!
Parthenia has our fields and mountains left.
Alph. Ay something 'twas my pipe was t' other day
So strangely out of tune, and in so hoarse a key.
Zeb. And I too this misfortune might have known
By some late signs, had my thoughts been my own.
My little goats as I to pasture led
When the grass rises from its dewy bed.
I wonder'd why the new born flowers hung down
Their languid heads, as if scorch'd by the sun.
The lilly and the rose to droop were seen,
And so did the immortal evergreen,
Parthenia – alas – was gone –
For thee sweet maid, lilly and rose did grieve,
The evergreen thy absence did perceive.
Asor. There grows a shady elm in our yonder grove
Where Philomel wou'd constantly repair,
Sweet Philomel, of all the joy and love
And with melodious accents fill the air.
When Parthenis was here, this shady tree,
Was never, never from her music free.
But now divine Parthenia is gone,

[1] = Renati Rapin "Carmina", Paris 1681

Silent and sad she wanders up and down,
And among thorns and lonely hedges makes her moan.
Alph. Whil'st thou fair nymph didst bless us with thy stay,
Each grove was sprightly, every wood was gay.
The boughs with birds, the caves with swains did ring,
And the shrill grasshopper about the field did sing.
But now each wood is silent as the grave,
Nor does the shepherd whistle in his cave,
Nor does the bird sit chirping on the bough,
Nor is the grasshopper to be heard now.
Zeb. The fields with living springs were fruitful made,
And every spring had his refreshing shade,
Sweet flowers to the bees were ne'er deny'd,
The fold with grass was constantly supplied.
Now Parthenis is gone, the industrious bee
Can't flowers procure with all his industry:
The folds want grass, the fields their living springs,
Nor have the mountains now their shady coverings:
Divine Parthenia! with thee we've lost
All the delights our rural life could boast.
Asor. My little goats were boldly wont to go
And climb the desert hills, my sheep would do so too:
Then happy sheep, the wolf the fold did spare,
The heat the infant trees, the rain the ripen'd ear.
Alph. Thou now perhaps sweet nymph art trave'ling o'er
Some craggy hills, unknown to thee before,
Whilst we sit here among the shady trees,
And swallow down each cool refreshing breese.
Zeb. Say you sweet western blasts that gently blow
And you fair rivers that as swiftly flow,
You who so often have been vocal made
By swains that pipe and sing under the shade;
Say, now when Phoebus holds the middle sky
Under what rock does sweet Parthenia lie?

Or through what coasts may I her wandrings trace?
Or in what fountain sees she now her lovely face?
Ah! Tho our way of life be plain and course[1]
Yet don't thou like thy country e'er the worse
Since 't 'as thy happy parent been and nurse.
Asor. Ah! where's that sweet retreat can thee detain,
If thou thy native country do'st disdain?
Here are pure springs, and o'er the springs are bowers,
Fine woods and fruit trees, and a world of flowers.
Alph. But why, fair nymph, would'st thou be absent now,
When the sweet strawberry raises up his head,
Like morning sun all delicately red,
And odorous blossoms spring from every bough?
Zeb. Don't you my sheep that yonder bank come near
'Tis to Parthenia sacred all that's there,
Nor would the grass be touch'd by any but by her.
Asor. Before fierce Boreas blow with's boisterous mouth,
Or rainy weather come on from the South,
Be sure Parthenia to return again,
Lest by the cold thou suffer, or the rain.
Alph. In a choice garden is reserv'd for thee,
Sweet marjoram, and a large myrtle tree;
Myrtles thou always lov'st, come then if now
Thou still lov'st flow'rs as thou wert wont to do.
Zeb. Ripe apples now hang dangling on the tree
Ready to drop, and only stay for thee.
The fig of thy delay too dost complain,
The tender fig, but let them both remain
'Till thou to thy dear Nazareth return again.
Asor. Return sweet nymph, and with thee thou shalt bring
All the delights and beauties of the Spring.
Fresh grass again shall on the mountain grow,
The rivers shall with milk and nectar flow,
The woods shall put on their green livery,

[1] = coarse

And Nature in her pomp shall wait on thee.
The country swains shall flowers and presents bring,
And I a violet garland for my offering.
With me shall Azarias come along
Who with a smooth–wrought pipe shall play the song;
The song that Israel's Shepherd as he stood
By Jordan's bank, play'd to the listning flood.
Alph. But if thou longer should'st our hopes deceive,
With rushes I'll a basket for thee weave;
Here thy own Nazareth I'll represent,
How all things here thy absence do lament;
The little goats thou wandring here shalt see
Mournful and sad, and all for want of thee.
The rivers which before flow'd swift and clear
As glad the image of thy face to bear,
Shall move benum'd and slow, whilest on each hand
Appears the thirsty and forsaken sand.
The corn shall droop and languish in the field,
The meadows no fresh grass or herb shall yield,
The fir–tree which with stately pride before,
Her curious shady locks towards heaven spread,
Shall now with down–cast boughs and pensive head,
Thy absence mourn, and thy return implore.
Thou round about shalt all things weeping see,
If tears in rush–work may decipher'd be.
Zeb. Preserve ye powers, if you don't us disdain,
The nymph, whilest she runs panting o'er the plain.
And while she's absent since she once had love
For these our fields, take care, ye powers above
That neither rivers do their banks o'erflow,
Nor storms the pastures spoil, or ripen'd corn o'erthrow.
Asor. From night–fires let our stalls – sweet nymph – be free,
Defend from heat the rose, from cold the myrtle–tree,

While rose and myrtle are belov'd by thee,
That if you chance to cast a longing eye
Back on these fields, now naked and forlorn,
We may have still some flowers left to supply
Garlands t' express our joy, and dresses you t' adorn.
Alph. Haste not, if through rough ways thy journey lye,
Haste not, the heat will prove an injury.
Let not the sun thy brighter beauties spoil:
Ah! why wilt thou undo thy self with too much toil?
Take pleasing shelter in some gentle shade
'Till the day slacken, and the heat be allay'd.
Zeb. Parthenia, why dost thou our hopes prolong?
Perhaps too some ill pipe, and worser song
Now grate thy ears, whil'st thy poor country swain
On the deaf winds bestows sweet lays in vain.
Hang there my pipe till she return, and be
A silent monument of my misery.
For what are songs or mirth without her company?
Azor. Our hills shall mourn while distant coasts you bless,
Anamis shall not dance nor Sabaris.
The fields, the naked fields no songs shall know,
And brooks their discontent by murmuring streams shall shew.
Thus did the swains the absent nymph lament,
The neighbouring woods to Heav'n the doleful accents sent.

THE TENTH ODE OF THE SECOND BOOK OF HORACE TRANSLATED

'Tis much the better way, believe me 'tis,
Not far to venture on the great abyss,
Nor yet from storms thy vessel to secure;
To touch too nigh upon the dangerous shore.

The golden mean, as she's too nice to dwell
Among the ruins of a filthy cell,
So is her modesty withall as great
To baulk the envy of a princely seat.

Th' ambitious winds with greater spite combine
To shock the grandeur of the stately pine.
The height of structures makes the ruin large,
And clouds against high hills their hottest bolts discharge.

An even well-pois'd mind, an evil state
With hope, a good with fear does moderate.
The Summer's pride, by Winter is brought down,
And flowers again the conquering season crown.

Take heart, nor of the laws of Fate complain,
Tho now 'tis cloudy, 'twill clear up again.
The bow Apollo does not always use
But with his milder lyre sometimes awakes the Muse.

Be life and spirit, when Fortune proves unkind,
And summon up the vigour of thy mind.
But when thou'rt driven by too officious gales,
Be wise, and gather in the swelling sails.

THE DISCOURAGEMENT

What wou'd the wise mens censure be,
I wonder, should they hear me say
I was resolv'd to throw my books away;
How would some scorn, and others pity me!
Sure he's in love, 'its for some charming Eve
That he like Adam paradise does leave.
This only difference would be
Between my great grandsire, and me,
That I my paradise forego
For want of appetite to know.

'Tis not that knowledge I despise;
No, you misconstrue my design;
Or that t' enthusiasm I incline,
And hope by inspiration to be wise.
'Tis not for this I bid my books adieu,
No, I love learning full as well as you,
And have the arts' great circle run
With as much vigour as the sun
His Zodiac treads, till t' other day
A thought surpris'd me in my way.

Thought I, for anything I know,
What we have stamp'd for science[1] here,
Does only the appearance of it wear,
And will not pass above, tho current here below;
Perhaps they've other rules to reason by,
And what's truth here, with them's absurdity.
We truth by a refracted ray
View, like the sun at ebb of day:
Whom the gross, treacherous atmosphere,
Makes where it is not, to appear.

Why then shall I with sweat and pain
Dig mines of disreputable ore?
My labour's certain, so is not my store,
I may hereafter unlearn all again.
Why then for truth do I my spirits waste,
When after all I may be gull'd at last?
So when the honest patriarch thought
With seven years labour he had bought
His Rachel's love, by morning light
He found the errour of the night.

Or grant some knowledge dwells below,
'Tis but for some few years to stay
Till I'm set loose from this dark house of clay,
And in an instant I shall all things know.
Then shall I learn t' accumulate degrees,
And be at once made master of all sciences.
What need I then great sums lay out,
And that estate with care forestall,
Which when few years are come about,
Into my hands of course will fall?

[1] = 1 Timothy 6:20

THE LXIII CHAPTER OF ISAIAH PARAPHRASED TO THE SIXTH VERSE

A Pindarique Ode

Strange scene of glory! am I well awake?
Or is't my Fancy's wild mistake?
It cannot be a dream, bright beams of light
Flow from the vision's face, and pierce my tender sight.
No common vision this, I see
Some marks of more than common majesty.
Who is this mighty hero, who?
With glories round His head, and terrour in His brow?
From Bozrah lo He comes, a scarlet dye
O'respreads His cloaths, and does outvy
The blushes of the morning sky.
Triumphant and victorious He appears,
And honour in His looks and habit wears:
How strong He treads, how stately does He go!
Pompous and solemn is His pace,
And full of majesty, as is His face.
Who is this mighty hero, Who?
'Tis I Who to my promise faithful stand,
I Who the powers of Death, Hell, and the Grave,
Have foil'd with this all-conquering hand,
I Who most ready am, and mighty too to save.

Why wear'st Thou then this scarlet dye?
Say mighty hero, why?
Why do Thy garments look all red
Like them that in the wine-fat tread?
The wine-press I alone have trod,
The vast unweildy frame, which long did stand

Unmov'd, and which no mortal force could e'er command,
The ponderous mass I ply'd alone
And with Me to assist were none;
A mighty task it was, worthy the Son of God.
Angels stood trembling at the dreadful sight,
Concern'd with what success I should go through
The work I undertook to do;
Inrag'd I put forth all My might
And down the engine press'd, the violent force
Disturb'd the universe, put Nature out of course.
The blood gush'd out in streams, and chequer'd o're
My garments with its deepest gore;
With ornamental drops bedeck'd I stood,
And writ My victory with My enemy's blood.

The day, the signal day is come
When of My enemies I must vengeance take;
The day when Death shall have its doom,
And the dark kingdom with its powers shall shake.
Fate in her kalendar mark'd out this day with red,
She folded down the iron leaf, and thus she said,
This day, if ought I can divine be true,
Shall for a signal victory
Be celebrated to posterity:
Then shall the Prince of Light descend
And rescue mortals from th' infernal fiend,
Break through his strongest forts, and all his host subdue.
This said, she shut the adamantin volume close
And wish'd she might the crouding years transpose;
So much she long'd to have the scene display,
And see the vast event of this important day.

And now in midst of the revolving years,
This great, this mighty one appears:
The faithful traveller the sun,
Has number'd out the days, and the set period run.
I lookt, and to assist was none,
My angelick guards stood trembling by,
But durst not venture nigh:
In vain too from My Father did I look
For help, My Father Me forsook.
Amaz'd I was to see
How all deserted Me.
I took My fury for My sole support
And with My single arm the conquest won,
Loud acclamations fill'd all Heaven's court,
The hymning guards above
Strain'd to an higher pitch of joy and love,
The great Jehovah prais'd, and His victorious Son.

THE ELEVATION

Take wing – my soul – and upwards bend thy flight,
To thy originary fields of light.
Here's nothing, nothing here below
That can deserve thy longer stay;
A secret whisper bids thee go
To purer air, and beams of native day.
Th' ambition of the towring lark out-vy,
And like him sing as thou dost upward fly.

How all things lessen which my soul before
Did with the groveling multitude adore!
Those pageant glories disappear,
Which charm and dazzle mortals eyes:
How do I in this higher sphere,
How do I mortals, with their joys despise!
Pure, uncorrupted element I breath,
And pity their gross atmosphere beneath.

How vile, how sordid here those trifles shew
That please the tenants of that ball below!
But ah! I've lost the little sight,
The scene's remov'd, and all I see
Is one confus'd dark mass of night.
What nothing was, what nothing seems to be:
How calm this region, how serene, how clear!
Sure I some strains of heavenly musick hear.

On, on, the task is easie now and light,
No steams of earth can here retard thy flight.
Thou needst not now thy strokes renew,
'Tis but to spread thy pinions wide,
And thou with ease my seat will view,
Drawn by the bent of the ethereal tide.
'Tis so I find; How sweetly on I move,
Nor let[1] by things below, nor help'd by those above!

[1] = hindered

But see, to what new region am I come?
I know it well, it is my native home.
Here led I once a life divine,
Which did all good, no evil know:
Ah! who wou'd such sweet bliss resign
For those vain shews which fools admire below?
'Tis true, but don't of folly past complain,
But joy to see these blest abodes again.

A good retrieve: but lo, while thus I speak,
With piercing rays, th' eternal day does break,
The beauties of the face divine,
Strike strongly on my feeble sight:
With what bright glories does it shine!
'Tis one immense and ever-flowing light.
Stop here my soul; thou canst not bear more bliss,
Nor can thy now rais'd palate ever relish less.

THE CURIOSITY

Unhappy state of mortals here below,
Whom unkind Heaven does inspire,
With such a constant, strong desire,
When they've such slender faculties, to know!
And yet we not content to bear the pain,
Of thirst unquencht and fruitless love,
With one more curse our ills improve,
And toil and drudge for what we ne're can gain.

With what strange frenzy are we all possest,
Contented ignorance to refuse,
And by laborious search to lose,
Not the enjoyment only, but our rest!
Something like ore does on the surface shine;
We taken with the specious shew,
With pains dig in the flattering mine
But all alas in vain, Truth lies more low.

The greatest knowledge we can ever gain
From studying Nature, Books, or Men,
Serves just t' employ dull hours; but then
It yields less pleasure than it costs us pain.
Besides, so short and treacherous is our age,
No sooner are we counted wise,
But envious Death shuts up our eyes;
Just as our part is learnt, we quit the stage.

Could I among the nobler spirits find
One that would lay aside his state,
And be my kind confederate,
That suddainly I might inrich my mind;
'Twould be some pleasure this, if happy I
Could once at ease sit and survey
And my great victory enjoy,
And – not as now – still labour on and dye.

THE 114th PSALM PARAPHRASED

When conquer'd by the plagues of Moses' rod
Th' Egyptian tyrant gave command
That Israel should depart his Land,
Israel the chosen family of God.
Among them dwelt the Holy One,
Juda His sanctuary, and Israel was His throne.

The sea beheld this scene, and did admire,
Each wave stood silently to see
The power of the Divinity;
They saw, and fled the dreadful guide of fire.
And Jordan too divided stood,
The priests the sacred ark bore through the yielding flood.

Mount Sinai with great horrour struck and dread
Forgot her weight, and in a trance
Like a light ram, did skip and dance;
She fear'd, and fain would hide her palsy head,
The hills their mother mountain saw,
The little hills, and like young sheep they stood in awe.

What made thee to retreat, thou mighty sea?
Tell me, for never any shore
Knew such a wondrous tide before,
And thou great Jordan; say, what ailèd thee?
Say sacred mount, what meant thy trance,
And you small under–hills, why did you skip and dance?

You need not think it shame to own your fear;
What you dismaid, the same would make
The universal fabrick shake;
The cause was great, for Jacob's God was there,
That God who did the rock subdue,
And made it melt in tears, tho' harder far than you.

THE 148th PSALM PARAPHRASED

O come let all created force conspire
A general hymn of praise to sing;
Join all ye creatures in one solemn quire,
And let your theme be Heaven's almighty King.

Begin ye blest attendants of His seat,
Begin your high seraphic lays,
'Tis just you should, your happiness is great,
And all you are to give again, is praise.

Ye glorious lamps that rule both night and day,
Bring your Allelujahs too;
To Him that tribute of devotion pay
Which once blind Superstition gave to you.

Thou first and fairest of material kind,
By whom His other works we see,
Subtile and active as pure thought and mind,
Praise Him that's elder, and more fair than thee.

Ye regions of the air His praises sing,
And all ye virgin waters there,
Do ye advantage to the consort bring,
And down to us the Allelujah bear,

In chaunting forth the great Jehovah's praise
Let these the upper consort fill;
He spake, and did you all from nothing raise;
As you did then, so now obey His will.

His will, that fix'd you in a constant state
And cut a track for Nature's wheel,
Here let it run said He, and make it Fate,
And where's that power which can this law repeal?

Ye powers that to th' inferiour world retain,
Join you now with the quire above.
And first ye dragons try an higher strain,
And turn your angry hissings into praise and love.

Let fire, hail, snow and vapours that ascend
Unlock'd by Phoebus' searching rays,
Let stormy winds ambitiously contend,
And all their wonted force imploy in praise,

Ye sacred tops which seem to brave the skies,
Rise higher, and when men on you
Religious rites perform and sacrifice,
With their oblations send your praises too.

Ye trees whose fruits both men and beasts consume
Be you in praises fruitful too;
Ye cedars, why have you such choice perfume
But that sweet incense should be made of you?

Ye beasts with all the humble creeping train
Praise Him that made your lot so high;
Ye birds who in a nobler province reign
Send up your praises higher than you fly.

Ye sacred heads, that wear imperial gold,
Praise Him that you with power arrays,
And you whose hands the scale of Justice hold,
Be just in this, and pay your debt of praise.

Let sprightly youth give vigour to the quire,
Each sex with another vye;
Let feeble Age dissolv'd in praise expire,
And infants too in hymns their tender voices try.

Praise Him ye saints who piety profess
And at His altar spend your days;
Ye seed of Israel your great patron bless,
'Tis manna this, for angels food is praise.

A PASTORAL ON THE DEATH OF HIS SACRED MAJESTY KING CHARLES THE SECOND

The speakers are *Menalcas, Thyrsis* and *Daphnis.*

Thyr.

What, sad Menalcas? Sure this pleasant shade
Was ne'er for such a mournful tenant made.
All things smile round thee, and throughout the grove
Nature displays a scene of joy and love.
But shepherd where's thy flock?
Sure they in some forbidden pastures stray
Whilst here in sighs thou numbrest out the day.
Men. Ah Thyrsis, thou could'st witness heretofore
What strange affection to my flock I bore.
Thou know'st my Thyrsis, the Arcadian plain
Could not afford a more industrious swain,
But I no longer now that mind retain.
Thyr. What change so great but what Love's power can make?
Menalcas does his kids, and tender lambs forsake.
So I, when slave to Galetia's eyes,
Did neither city nor the country prize,
But all their sports, and my flock too despise.
Hang thou my pipe – said I, on yonder tree,
For then – alas – I had no taste for melody.
Obscurely in thick woods I sate alone,
And sigh'd in consort to the turtle's moan.
Men. 'Tis not fond Love that causes my distress;
No Thyrsis, you'r mistaken in your guess.
The glorious prize I have in triumph born,
I am no longer now Alexis scorn.
Or if I were, I now could be unmoved

At every scornful glance, nor care where e'er he loved.
A nearer grief preys on my spirits now,
And I beneath a heavier burthen bow.
The gentle god of the Arcadian plains
Pan that regards the sheep, Pan that regards the swains,
Great Pan is dead –
Throughout the fields the doleful tidings ran,
A swoon seiz'd all the shepherds at the death of Pan.
Of Pan – But see the rest that tree will shew
Which bears the sad inscription of my woe,
Where, with the bark my sorrows too will grow.
Thyr. How shepherd, is it by Fame's trumpet said
That Pan the best of all the gods is dead?
Whom oft w' adored, and whom because we knew
As good as they, we thought him as immortal too?
'Tis strange; but omens now I find are true,
In yonder copse a shady oak there stood,
Stately, well rooted, and it self a wood;
Her branches o'er the inferiour trees were spread,
Who all ador'd her as their soveraign head:
Hither, when heated by the guide of Day,
While their young wanton goats did skip and play.
Hither the swains would constantly repair,
Here sing, and in the ample shade drink fresher air.
This tree when I my goats to pasture drove,
While all was clear above, and still, through the grove,
Struck by some secret force fall down I saw,
The wood-nymphs all were seiz'd with wonder, grief, and awe.
Nor had I left this ruin far behind,
When lo – strange sight – a nightingal I find,
Which from brisk airs, enlivening all the grove
Coo'd on a suddain like a mournful dove.
Amaz'd I stand, and on my pipe essay

With some brisk song her sorrows to allay;
But all in vain. She from the lofty tree
Kept on her sad complaint, and mourn'd and droop'd like thee.

Men. And why these slighter things dost thou relate?
Nature herself perceiv'd Pan's mighty fate.
She fainted when he drew his latest breath,
And almost sympathiz'd with him to death.
Each field put on a languid dying face
The sheep not minding food, with tears bedew'd the grass.
The lyons too in tears their grief confest,
And savage bears, Pan's enemies profest.
The nymphs all wept, and all the noble train
Of deitys that frequent the court of Pan.
Eccho, that long by nought but voice was known,
In sounds repeated others woes, but wept her own.
Th' Arcadians mourn'd, and press'd beneath the weighty care
With cruelty they charg'd the gods and every star.

Thyr. And well they might; Heaven could not shew a deity
More mild, more good to his votaries than he.
He was all love, all peace, all clemency;
H' allur'd the love, and melted down the hate
Of all: he had no enemy but Fate.
Pan kept the fields, from wolves secur'd the stall,
He guarded both the humble shrubs and cedars tall.
The Summer's heat obey'd Pan's gentle hand,
And Winter winds blew soft at his command,
He blest the swains with sheep, and fruitful made their land.
Weep shepherds, and in pomp your grief express,
The ground with flowers, yourselves with cypress dress,
Let the Arcadians in a solemn train

March slowly on, let mournful accents fill the plain,
Do this at least in memory of Pan.
  Daph. But why this vain expence of tears and breath?
D' ye think Pan lost and swallowed up in death?
He lives, and with a pleas'd and wondering eye
Contemplates the new beauties of the sky.
Whence on these fields he casts propitious rays,
Now greater than our sorrow, greater than our praise.
I saw – for why mayn't I rehearse the sight –
Just as the stars were kindled by the queen of Night
Another new–made milky way appear,
I saw, and wonder'd what event it might prepare.
When lo great Pan amaz'd my trembling sight,
As through th' æthereal plains he took his flight
Deck'd round with rays, and darting streams of light.
Triumphant was his march, a sacred throng
Of gods inclos'd him, Pan was all their song,
The sky still brighten'd as they went along.
  Men. Thy vision be all truth –
But who shall now the royal sheep–crook hold,
Who patronize the fields, who now secure the fold?
  Daph. Discharge that care, the royal stock does yield
Another Pan to patronize the field,
An heir of equal conduct does the scepter sway,
One who long nurtured in the pastoral way,
In peace will govern the Arcadian plains,
Defend the slender flocks, and cheer the drooping swains.
  Thyr. Come then, let's tune the pipe t' a brisker key,
Let's with a dance our sorrows chase away,
And to new Pan in sports devote the day.

SATIETY

Haste on dull Time, thy wingèd minutes haste,
I care not now how soon thou bring'st my last.
But what I've liv'd I plainly know,
The total sum of all below.
The days to come, altho they promise more,
I know will be as false as those that went before.

The best of life tho once, enjoy'd, is vain,
And why ye Powers the self-same o'er again?
The comedy's so dull, I fear,
'Twill not a second acting bear.
No, I've enough; I cannot like the sun,
Each day the self-same stage, and still unwearied run.

What cruel laws are these that me confine,
Thus still to dig in a deceitful mine?
Be just ye Powers, my soul set free,
Give her her native liberty,
'Tis 'gainst the stage's law to force my stay,
I've seen an act or two and do not like the Play.

THE REPLY

Since you desire of me to know
Who's the wise man, I'll tell you who.
Not he whose rich and fertile mind
Is by the culture of the arts refin'd;
Who has the chaos of disorder'd thought

By Reason's light, to form and method brought.
Who with a clear and piercing sight
Can see through niceties as dark as night,
You err, if you think this is he,
Though seated on the top of the Porphyrian tree.[1]

Nor is it he to whom kind Heaven
A secret cabala has given
T' unriddle the mysterious text
Of Nature, with dark comments more perplext.
Or to decypher her clean writ and fair,
But most confounding puzling character.
That can through all her windings trace
This slippery wanderer, and unveil her face.
Her inmost mechanism view,
Anatomize each part, and see her through and through.

Nor he that does the science know
Our only certainty below,
That can from problems dark and nice
Deduce truths worthy of a sacrifice.
Nor he that can confess the stars, and see
What's writ in the black leaves of Destiny.
That knows their laws, and how the sun,
His daily and his annual stage does run;
As if he did to them dispence,
Their motions, and their sate supream intelligence.

Nor is it he – although he boast
Of wisdom, and seem wise to most –
Yet 'tis not he, whose busy pate

[1] = the olive tree growing in the cave of the Nymphs (Homer)

Can dive into the deep intrigues of State.
That can the great Leviathan controul,
Manage and rule't, as if he were its soul.
The wisest king thus gifted was,
And yet did not in these true wisdom place.
Who then is by this wise man meant?
He that can want all this, and yet can be content.

MY ESTATE

How do I pity that proud wealthy clown,
That does with scorn on my low state look down!
Thy vain contempt dull earth-worm cease,
I won't for refuge fly to this,
That none of Fortune's blessings can,
Add any value to the man.
This all the wise acknowledge to be true;
But know I am as rich, more rich than you.

While you a spot of Earth possess with care,
Below the notice of the Geographer,
I by the freedom of my soul,
Possess, nay more, enjoy the whole;
To th' Universe a claim I lay;
Your writings shew perhaps you'll say,
That's your dull way, my title runs more high,
'Tis by the charter of Philosophy.

From a firmer title I derive
Than all your courts of Law doth ever give.
A title that more firm doth stand
Than does even your very land,
And yet so generous and free,
That none will e'er bethink it me,
Since my possessions tend to no man's loss,
I all enjoy, yet nothing I ingross.

Throughout the works divine I cast my eye,
Admire their beauty, and their harmony,
I view the glorious host above,
And Him that made them, praise and love,
The flowery meads and fields beneath,
Delight me with their odorous breath.
Thus is my joy by you not understood
Like that of God, when He said all was good.

Nay – what you'd think less likely to be true –
I can enjoy what's yours much more than you,
Your meadow's beauty I survey,
Which you prize only for its hay.
There can I sit beneath a tree,
And write an ode or elegy.
What to you care, does to me pleasure bring,
You own the cage, I in it sit and sing.

THE CONQUEST

In power or wisdom to contend with thee
Great God, who but a Lucifer would dare?
Our strength is but infirmity,
And when we this perceive our sight's most clear:
But yet I will not be excell'd thought I,
In love, in love I'll with my Maker vy.
I view'd the glories of Thy seat above,
And thought of every grace and charm divine,
And further to increase my love
I measured all the heights and depths of Thine.
Thus there broke forth a strong and vigorous flame,
And almost melted down my mortal frame.

But when Thy bloody sweat and death I view,
I own – dear Lord –the conquest of thy love.
Thou dost my highest flights outdo,
I in a lower orb, and slower move.
Thus in this strife's a double weakness shewn,
Thy love I cannot equal, nor yet bear my own.

THE IMPATIENT

What envious laws are those of Fate,
Which fix a gulph – blest souls – 'twixt us and you!
How 'twou'd refresh and chear our mortal state,
When our dejected looks confess
The emptiness of earthly bliss,
Could we in this black night your brighter glories view!

Vain comfort when I thus complain,
To hear the wise and solemn gravely say,
Your grief and curiosity restrain,
Death will e'er long this bar remove,
And bring you to the blest above,
Till then with this great prospect all your longings stay.

But ah the joy peculiar here
Does from the greater excellence arise,
'Twill be worth nothing in an equal sphere.
Let me your noble converse have
Blest spirits, on this side the grave,
I shall hereafter be as great as you, as wise.

Besides, when plung'd in bliss divine
I shall not taste, nor need this lesser joy.
What comfort then does from this prospect shine.
'Tis just as if in depth of night,
You rob a traveller of his light;
And promise to restor't when 'tis clear day.

CONTENT

I bless my stars I envy none,
Not great, not wealthy, no nor yet the wise;
I've learn't the art to like my own,
And what I can't attain to, not to prize.
Vast tracts of learning I descry
Beyond the sphere perhaps of my activity,

And yet I'm ne'er the more concern'd at this,
Than for the gems that lye in the profound abyss.

Should I my proper lot disdain,
As long as further good eclipses mine,
I may t' Eternity complain,
And in the mansions of the blest repine.
There shall I numbers vast espy
Of forms more excellent, more wise, more blest than I.
I shall not then lament my unequal fate,
And why should larger prospects now molest my state?

Where all in equal stations move
What place for harmony can there be found?
The lower spheres with those above
Agree, and dance as free and briskly round.
Degrees of essences conspire
As well as various notes t' accomplish Heaven's quire.
Thus will I have't below, nor will I care
So the result be harmony, what part I bear.

AGAINST KNOWLEDGE

Well let it be the censure of the wise,
That wisdom none but fools despise:
I like not what they gravely preach
And must another doctrin teach,
Since all's so false and vain below,
There's nought so indiscreet as this, to know.

The thoughtless, dull and less discerning mind
No flaws in earthly joys can find,
He closes with what courts his sight,
All coin will pass by his dim light.
Though often baulk't, he hopes for rest,
Sleeps on and dreams, and is in error blest.

But he that has refin'd and high–rais'd sense,
Can nothing taste but excellence.
Nor can he Nature's faults supply,
By Fancy's happy imag'ry.
He sees that all fruition's vain,
Can't taste the present, nor yet trust again.

Our joys, like tricks, do all on cheats depend,
And when once known, are at an end.
Happy and wise, two blessings are
Which meet not in this mortal sphere;
Let me be ignorant below,
And when I've solid good, then let me know.

SEEING A GREAT PERSON LYING IN STATE

Well now I needs must own
That I hate greatness more and more;
'Tis now a just abhorence grown
What was antipathy before:
What other ills I could dispence,

And acquiesce in providence.
But let not Heaven my patience try
With this one plague, lest I repine and dye.

I knew indeed before.
That 'twas the great man's wretched fate,
While with the living to endure
The vain impertinence of State;
But sure thought I, in death he'll be
From that and other troubles free:
What e'er his life, he then will lye
As free, as undisturb'd, as calm as I.

But 'twas a gross mistake;
Honour, that too officious ill,
Wont even his breathless corps forsake,
But haunts and waits about him still.
Strange persecution, when the grave
Can't the distressèd martyr save!
What remedy can there avail
Where death the great catholicon does fail?

Thanks to my stars that I
Am with so low a fortune blest,
That what e're blessings Fate deny,
I'm sure of privacy and rest.
'Tis well; thus lone I am content,
And rest as in my element.
Then Fate, if you'll appear my friend,
Force me not 'gainst my nature to ascend.

No, I would still be low,
Or else I would be very high,
Beyond the state which mortals know,
A kind of semi–deity.
So of the regions of the air
The highest and lowest quiet are,
But 'tis the middle height I fear,
For storms and thunder are ingendred there.

SECOND CHAPTER OF THE CANTICLES FROM VERSE 10 TO 13

'Twas my beloved spoke,
I know his charming voice, I heard Him say,
Rise up, My love, My fairest one awake,
Awake, and come away.

The Winter all is past
And stormy winds that with such rudeness blew;
The heavens are no longer overcast,
But try to look like you.

The flowers their sweets display,
The birds in short preludiums tune their throat,
The turtle in low murmurs does essay
Her melancholy note.

The fruitful vineyards make
An odorous smell; the fig looks fresh and gay;
Arise my love, my fairest one awake,
Awake and come away.

TO A FRIEND IN HONOUR

Some thoughtless heads perhaps admire[1] to see
That I so little to your titles bow;
But wonder not my friend, I swear to me
You were as great before as now.
Honour to you does nothing give,
Tho' from your worth much lustre she receive.

Your native glory does so far out–do
That of the sphere wherein you move,
That I can nothing but your self in you
Observe, admire, esteem or love.
You are a diamond set in gold,
The curious, the rich stone, not this behold.

All that to your late honour you can owe
Is only that you're brought in view;
You don't begin to have, but men to know,
Your votaries are increas'd, not you.
So the sun's height adds not t' his light,
But only does expose him more to sight.

[1] = wonder

To some whose native worth more dimly shin'd
Honour might some improvement give,
As metals which the sun has less refin'd
A value from their stamp receive.
But you like gold pass, for no more
Tho stamp'd, than for your weight you wou'd before.

A DIVINE HYMN ON THE CREATION

Awake my lyre, and thy sweet forces joyn
With me to sing an hymn divine;
Let both our strains in pleasing numbers flow,
But see, thy strings with tediousness and pain
Arise into a tuneful strain;
How canst thou silent lye?
The Universe is harmony,
Awake, and move by sympathy,
My heart's already tun'd, O why art thou so slow?

Jehovah is our theme, th' Eternal King,
Whose praise admiring angels sing,
They see with steddy and attentive eyes,
His naked beauties, and from vision raise
To wondrous heights their love and praise.
We mortals only view
His back–parts, and that darkly too;
We must fall short, what shall we do?
But neither too can they up to His grandeur rise.

No power can justly praise Him but must be
As great, as infinite as He;
He comprehends His boundless Self alone,
Created minds too shallow are and dim,
His works to fathom, much more Him.
Our praise at height will be
Short by a whole infinity,
Of His all glorious Deity,
He cannot have the full, and stands in need of none.

He can't be less, nor can He more receive,
But stands one fix'd superlative.
He's in Himself compendiously blest;
We, acted by the weights of strong desire
To good without ourselves aspire,
We're always moving hence
Like lines from the circumference,
To some more inlodg'd excellence,
But He is one unmov'd self–centr'd point of rest.

Why then, if full of bliss that ne're could cloy,
Would He do ought but still enjoy?
Why not indulge His self–sufficing state,
Live to Himself at large, calm and secure,
A wise eternal epicure?
Why six days work, to frame
A monument of praise and fame
To Him whose bliss is still the same?
What need the wealthy coin, or He that's blest create?

Almighty love the fairest gem that shone
All round, and half made up His throne.
His favourite and darling excellence,
Whom oft He would His royal virtue stile,
And view with a peculiar smile,
Love movèd Him to create
Beings that might participate
Of their Creator's happy state,
And that good which He could not heighten, to dispence.

How large thy empire, Love, how great thy sway!
Omnipotence does thee obey.
What complicated wonders in thee shine!
He that t' infinity it self is great
Has one way to be greater yet;
Love will the method shew,
'Tis to impart; what is't that thou
O sovereign passion can'st not do?
Thou mak'st divinity it self much more divine.

With pregnant love full–fraught, the great Three–One,
Would now no longer be alone,
Love, gentle love, unlockt His fruitful breast,
And 'woke the ideas that there dormant lay,
Awak'd their beauties they display:
Th' Almighty smil'd to see
The comely form and harmony
Of His eternal imag'ry;
He saw 'twas good and fair, and th' infant platform blest.

Ye seeds of being, in whose fair bosoms dwell
The forms of all things possible;
Arise, and your prolific force display;
Let a fair issue in your moulds be cast
To fill in part this empty waste.
He spake. The empty space
Immediately in travail was
And soon brought forth a formless mass:
First matter came undress'd, she made such haste t' obey.

But soon a plastick spirit did ferment
The liquid dusky element.
The mass harmoniously begins to move,
"Let there be light" said God! 'twas said and done,
The mass dipt through with brightness, shone.
Nature was pleas'd to see
This feature of divinity,
Th' Almighty smil'd as well as she,
He own'd His likeness there, and did His first-born love.

But lo, I see a goodly frame arise
Vast folding orbs, and azure skies,
With lucid whirl-pools the vast arch does shine,
The sun by day shews to each world his light,
The stars stand sentinel by night.
In midst of all is spread
That pondrous bulk whereon we tread,
But where is its foundation laid?
'Tis pompous all and great, and worthy hands divine.

Thy temple's built great God but where is he,
That must admire both it and Thee?
Ope one scene more, my Muse, bless and adore,
See there in solemn councel and debate
The great divine triumvirate.
The rest one word obey'd
'Twas done almost before 'twas said;
But man was not so cheaply made,
To make the world was great, but t' epitomise it more.

Th' accomplish'd work stands His severe review
Whose judgement's most exactly true.
All things are good, said God, they answer well
Th' ideas which within Me dwell;
Th' angelick voices, joyn
Their praise to the applause divine,
The morning stars in hymns combine,
And as they sung and play'd, the jocant[1] orbs danc't round.

With this Thy quire divine, great God I bring
My eucharistick offering.
I cannot here sing more exalted layes,
But what's defective now I will supply
When I enjoy Thy deity.
Then may'st thou sleep my lyre,
I shall not then thy help require,
Diviner thoughts will then me fire
Than thou, tho' play'd on by an angel's hand, canst raise.

[1] = jocund

PLATO'S TWO CUPIDS

The heart of man's a living butt,
At which two different archers shoot,
Their shafts are pointed both with fire,
Both wound our hearts with hot desire.

In this they differ, he that lyes
A sacrifice t' his mistress eyes,
In pain does live, in pain expire,
And melts and drops before the fire.

But he that flames with love divine,
Does not in th' heat consume, but shine.
H' enjoys the fire that round him lies,
Serenely lives, serenely dies.

So devils and damnèd souls in Hell
Fry in the fire with which they dwell;
But angels suffer not the same,
Altho their vehicles be flame.

The heart whose fire's divine and chaste,
Is like the bush that did not waste.
Moses beheld the flame with fear,
That wasted not, for God was there.

A WISH

Whatever blessing you my life deny,
Grant me kind Heaven this one thing when I dye.
I charge thee guardian spirit hear,
And as thou lov'st me, further this my prayer.

When I'm to leave this grosser sphere, and try
Death, that amazing curiosity,
When just about to breathe my last,
Then when no mortal joy can strike my taste,

Let me soft melting strains of musick hear,
Whose dying sounds may strike death to my ear;
Gently the bands of life unty,
Till in sweet raptures I dissolve and dye.

How soft and easie my new birth will be,
Help'd on by Musick's gentle midwifery!
And I who 'midst these charms expire,
Shall bring a soul well tun'd to heav'ns quire.

TO DR. HENRY MORE. AN ODE

Go Muse, go hasten to the cell of Fame,
– Thou knows't her reverend aweful seat –
It stands hard by your blest retreat,
Go, with a brisk alarm assault her ear,

Bid her her loudest trump prepare,
To sound a more than human name;
A name more excellent and great
Than she could ever publish yet;
Tell her she need not stay till Fate shall give
A license to his works, and bid them live.
His worth now shines through Envy's base alloy,
'Twill fill her loudest trump and all her breath employ.

Learning, which long like an inchanted land,
Did human force and art defie,
And stood the virtuoso's best artillery,
Which nothing mortal could subdue,
Has yielded to this hero's fatal hand,
By him is conquer'd, held, and peopled too.
Like seas that border on the shore
The Muses' suburbs some possession knew,
But like the deep abyss their inner store
Lay unpossess'd, till seiz'd and own'd by you:
Truth's outer courts were trod before,
Sacred was her recess, that Fate reserv'd for More.

Others in Learning's chorus bear their part
And the great work distinctly share:
Thou our great catholick professor art,
All science is annex'd to thy unerring chair.
Some lesser Synods of the wise
The Muses kept in Universities;
But never yet till in thy soul
Had they a councel oecumenical,
An abstract they'd a mind to see
Of all their scatter'd gifts, and summ'd them up in thee.
Thou hast the arts' whole Zodiack run,

And fathom'st all that here is known.
Strange restless curiosity,
Adam himself came short of thee,
He tasted of the fruit, thou bear'st away the tree.

Whilst to be great the most aspire,
Or with low souls to raise their fortunes higher.
Knowledge the chiefest treasure of the blest,
Knowledge the wise man's best request,
Was made thy choice; for this thou hast declin'd
A life of noise, impertinence, and state,
And what e're else the Muses hate,
And made it thy own business to inrich thy mind.
How calm thy life, how easie, how secure,
Thou intellectual epicure.
Thou as another Solomon hast try'd
All Nature through, and nothing to thy soul deny'd.
Who can two such examples shew?
He all things try'd t' enjoy, and you all things to know.

By Babel's curse and our contracted span.
Heaven thought to check the swift career of man.
And so it prov'd till now, our age
Is much too short to run so long a stage.
And to learn words is such a vast delay,
That we're benighted e'r we come half way.
Thou with unusual haste driv'st on,
And dost even Time itself out–run.
No hindrance can retard thy course,
Thou rid'st the Muses' wingèd horse;
Thy stage of Learning ends e'r that of life be done.
There's now no work left for thy accomplish'd mind,
But to survey thy conquests, and inform mankind.

THE PASSION OF THE VIRGIN MOTHER, BEHOLDING THE CRUCIFIXION OF HER DIVINE SON

Nigh to the fatal and yet sovereign wood,
Which crowds of wondring angels did surround,
Devoutly sad the holy mother stood,
And view'd her Son, and sympathiz'd with every wound.

Angelick pity in her mournful face,
Like rays of light, through a watry cloud did shine;
Two mighty passions in her breast took place,
And like her Son, sh' appear'd half human, half divine.

She saw a blacker and more tragic scene,
Than e'r the sun before, or then would see;
In vain did Nature draw her dusky screen,
She saw, and wept, and felt the dreadful agony.

Grief in the abstract sure can rise no higher
Than that which this deep tragedy did move;
She saw in tortures and in shame, expire
Her Son, her God, her Worship and her Love.

That sacred head, which all divine and bright,
Struck with deep awe, the votaries of the East,
To which a star paid tributary light,
Which the – then joyful – mother kiss'd, ador'd and blest.

That head which angels with pure light had crown'd,
Where wisdom's seat and oracle was plac'd;
Whose air divine threw's traitors to the ground,
She saw with pointed circles of rude thorns embrac'd.

Those hands whose sovereign touch were wont to heal
All wounds and hurts that others did endure,
Did now the piercings of rough iron feel,
Nor could the wounded heart of his mother cure.

No, no, it bled to see His body torn
With nails, and deck'd with gems of purple gore;
On four great wounds to see Him rudely born,
Whom oft her arms a happy burthen found before.

It bled to hear that voice of grief and dread,
Which the Earth's pillars and foundations shook;
Which rent the rocks, and woke the sleeping dead,
My God, my God, O why, why hast Thou me forsook?

And can the tide of sorrow rise more high?
Her melting face stood thick with tears to view,
Like those of heaven His setting glories dye,
As flowers left by the sun are charg'd with evening dew.

But see Grief spreads her empire still more wide,
Another spring of tears begins to flow,
A barbarous hand wounds His now senseless side:
And death that ends the Son's renews the mother's woe.

She sees now by the rude inhuman stroke,
The mystic river flow, and in her breast
Wonders, by what strange figure th' angel spoke,
When amongs't all the daughters he pronounc'd her blest,

Thus far did Nature, Pity, Fear and Love,
And all the passions their strong efforts try,
But still tho dark below, 'twas clear above,
She had – as once her son – her strengthning angel by.

Gabriel the chiefest of th' Almighty's train
That first with happy tidings blest her ear,
Th' archangel Gabriel, was sent again,
To stem the tide of grief, and qualifie her fear.

A large prospective wrought by hands divine
He set before her first enlightned eye,
'Twas hewn out of the heaven christalline,
One of whose ends did lessen, th' other magnifie.

With that His sufferings he expos'd to sight,
With that His glories he did represent;
The weight of this made th' other seem but light,
She saw the mighty odds, ador'd and was content.

DAMON AND PYTHIAS: OR, FRIENDSHIP IN PERFECTION

Pyth.

'Tis true – my Damon – we as yet have been
Patterns of constant love, I know;
We have stuck so close no third could come between,
But will it – Damon – will it still be so?

Da. Keep your love true, I dare engage that mine
Shall like my soul immortal prove.
In friendship's orb how brightly shall we shine
Where all shall envy, none divide our love!

Pyth. Death will; when once – as 'tis by Fate design'd –
T' Elysium you shall be remov'd,
Such sweet companions there no doubt you'll find,
That you'll forget that Pythias e'r you lov'd.

Da. No, banish all such fears; I then will be
Your friend and guardian angel too.
And tho with more refin'd society
I'll leave Elysium to converse with you.

Pyth. But grant that after Fate you still are kind,
You cannot long continue so;
When I, like you, become all thought and mind,
By what mark then shall we each other know?

Da. With care on your last hour I will attend,
And lest like souls should me deceive,
I closely will embrace my new-born friend,
And never after my dear Pythias leave.

THE INDIFFERENCY

Whether 'tis from stupidity or no,
I know not; but I ne're could find
Why I one thought or passion should bestow
On fame, that gaudy idol of mankind.
Call me not Stoick; no, I can pursue
Things excellent with as much zeal as you:
But here I own my self to be
A very luke-warm votary.

Should thousand excellencies in me meet,
And one bright constellation in me frame,
'Tis still as mens phantastick humours hit
Whether I'm written in the book of Fame.
So tho the sun be ne're so fair and bright,
And shine with uninterrupted light,
'Tis as the clouds disposèd are,
E're he can paint his image there.

The world is seldom to true merit just,
Through envy or through ignorance,
True worth, like valour, oft lies hid in dust,

While some false hero's grac'd with a romance.
The true God's altar oft neglected lies,
When idols have perfumes and sacrifice.
And though the true One some adore,
Yet those that do blaspheme are more.

Yet grant that merit were of fame secure,
What's reputation, what is praise?
Who'd one day's toil, or sleepless night endure,
Such a vain Babel of esteem to raise?
Pleas'd with his hidden worth, the great and wise
Can, like his God, this foreign good despise;
Whose happiness would n'er be less.
Tho none were made to praise or bless.

Even I who dare not rank myself with those
Who pleas'd into themselves retire,
Find yet in great applauses less repose,
And do fame less, less than my self admire.
Let her loud trumpet sound me far and near,
Th' Antipodes will never of me hear.
Or were I known throughout this ball,
I've but a point, when I have all.

Then as for glory which comes after Fate,
All that can then of me be said,
I value least of all, it comes too late:
'Tis like th' embalming of the senseless dead.
Others with pleasure, what me labour cost,
May read, and praise; but to me all is lost.
Just as the sun no joy does find
In that his light, which chears mankind.

Or should I after Fate has closed my eyes,
Should I my living glories know,
My wiser, improv'd soul will then despise
All that poor mortals say or think below.
Even they who of men's ignorance before
Complain'd, because few did their works adore,
Will then the self same censure raise,
Not from their silence, but their praise.

Or grant 'twou'd pleasure bring to know that I
After my death live still in fame;
Those that admire me too must shortly dye,
And then where's my memorial, where my name?
My fame, tho longer liv'd, yet once shall have
Like me, its death, its funeral, its grave.
This only difference will remain,
I shall, that never rise again.

Death and destruction shall e're long deface
The world, the work of hands divine,
What pillars then, or monuments of brass
Shall from the general ruin rescue mine?
All then shall equal be; I care not then
To be a while the talk and boast of men.
This only grant, that I may be
Prais'd by Thy angels; Lord, and Thee.

THE INFIRMITY

In other things I ne're admir'd to see
Men injured by extremity.
But little thought in happiness
There might be danger of excess:
At least I thought there was no fear
Of ever meeting with too much on't here.

But now these melting sounds strike on my sense
With such a powerfull excellence;
I find that happiness may be
Screw'd up to such extremity,
That our too feeble faculties
May not be said t' enjoy, but suffer bliss.

So frail's our mortal state, we can sustain,
A mighty bliss no more than pain.
We lose our weak precarious breath,
Tortur'd or tickled unto death.
As sprights and angels alike fright,
With too much horror, or with too much light.

Alas! I'm over–pleas'd, what shall I do
The painful joy to undergo?
Temper your too melodious song,
Your dose of bliss is much too strong;
Like those that too rich cordials have,
It don't so much revive, as make me rave.

What cruelty 'twou'd be still to confine
A mortal ear to airs divine?
The curse of Cain you have on me,
Inverted by your harmony,
For since with that you charm'd my ear,
My bliss is much too great for me to bear.

Relieve this paroxysm of delight,
And let it be less exquisite.
Let down my soul; 'tis too high set;
I am not ripe for Heaven yet.
Give me a region more beneath,
The element's too fine for me to breath.

THE ARREST

Whither so fast fond Passion dost thou rove,
Licentious and unconfin'd?
Sure this is not the proper sphere of love,
Obey, and be not deaf, as thou art blind.
All is so false and treacherous here,
That I must love with caution, and enjoy with fear.

Contract thy sails, lest a too gusty blast
Make thee from shore launch out too far;
Weigh well this ocean, e're thou make such haste,
It has a nature very singular.
Men of the treacherous shore complain
In other seas, but here most danger's in the main.

Should'st thou, my soul, indulge thy forward love,
And not controul its headlong course,
The object in th' enjoyment vain will prove,
And thou on nothing fall with all thy force.
So th' eager hawk makes sure of's prize,
Strikes with full might, but overshoots himself and dyes.

Or should'st thou with long search on something light
That might content and stay thy hand,
All good's here wing'd, and stands prepar'd for flight,
'Twill leave thee reaching out in vain, behind.
Then when inconstant Fate thou'st proved,
Thou'lt sigh, and say with tears, I wish I ne're had loved.

Well then ye softer Powers, that love command
And wound our breasts with pleasing smart,
Gage well your launce, and bear a steddy hand,
Lest it run in too deep into my heart.
Or if you're fixed in your design
Deeply to wound my heart, wound it with love divine.

TO THE MEMORY OF MY DEAR NEECE, M.C.

By tears to ease my grief I've try'd,
And philosophick med'cins have applied;
From books and company I've sought relief,
I've used all spells and charms of art,
To lay this troubler of my heart,

I have, yet I'm still haunted by my grief.
These give some ease, but yet I find
'Tis poetry at last must cure my mind.

Come then, t' asswage my pain I'll try,
By the sweet magick of thy harmony.
Begin my Muse, but 'twill be hard I know
For thee my genius to screw
To heights that to my theme are due,
The weight of grief has set my soul so low.
To grace her death my strains should be
As far above mortality as she.

Is she then dead, and can it be
That I can live to write her elegy?
I hoped, since 'twas not to my soul deny'd
To sympathise in all the pain
Which she, tho long, did well sustain,
T' have carried on the sympathy and dy'd.
But Death was so o're pleas'd I see
At this rich spoil, that she neglected me.

Yet has she, of all things made me bare,
But life, nor was it kindness here to spare.
So when th' Almighty would t' inform mankind
His Eastern hero's patience try
With the extreams of misery;
He gave this charge to the malicious fiend;
Of all life's blessings him deprive,
Vex him with all thy plagues, but let him live.[1]

[1] = Job 2:6

Yet I will live – sweet soul – to save
Thy name, since thee I cannot from the grave.
I will not of this burthen life complain
Tho tears than verses faster flow,
Tho I am plung'd in grief and woe,
And like th' inspirèd Sybils write in pain.
To dye for friends is thought to be
Heroick, but I'll life endure for thee.

'Tis just, since I in thee did live
That thou shouldst life and fame from me receive.
But how shall I this debt of justice pay?
The colours of my poetry
Are all too dead to copy thee,
'Twill be abuse the best that I can say.
Nature that wrought thy curious frame
Will find it hard to draw again the same.

In council the Almighty sate
When He did man his master–piece create,
His agent Nature did the same for thee;
In making thee she wrought for fame,
And with slow progress drew thy frame,
As he that painted for Eternity.
In her best mould she did thee cast,
But thou wast over–wrought, and made too fine to last.

Thy soul the saint of this fair shrine,
Was pure without alloy, and all divine.
Active and nimble as æthereal light,
Kind as the angels are above

Who live on harmony and love,
The rays thou shott'st were warm, as well as bright:
So mild, so pleasing was thy fire,
That none could envy, and all must admire.

Sickness, to whose strong seige resign
The best of natures, did but set forth thine.
Wisely thou didst thy passions all controul,
And like a martyr in the fire
Devout and patient did'st expire,
Pains could expel, but none untune thy soul.
Thou bore'st them all so moderately
As if thou mean'st to teach how I should mourn for thee.

No wonder such a noble mind
Her way again to Heaven so soon could find.
Angels, as 'tis but seldom they appear,
So neither do they make long stay:
They do but visit and away,
'Tis pain for them t' endure our too gross sphere.
We could not hope for a reprieve.
She must dye soon, that made such haste to live.

The angels too did covet thee
T' advance their love, their bliss, their harmony.
They'd lately made an anthem to their King,
An anthem which contain'd a part
All sweet, and full of heavenly art,
Which none but thy harmonious soul could sing.
'Twas all heaven's vote thou should'st be gone
To fill th' Almighty's quire, and to adorn His throne.

Others when gone t' eternal rest
Are said t' augment the number of the blest.
Thou dost their very happiness improve;
Out of the croud they single thee,
Fond of thy sweet society.
Thou wast our darling, and art so above.
Why should we of thy loss complain
Which is not only thine, but Heaven's gain?

There dost thou sit in bliss and light,
Whilst I thy praise in mournful numbers write.
There dost thou drink at Pleasure's virgin spring,
And find'st no leisure in thy bliss
Ought to admire below, but this.
How can I mourn, when thou dost anthems sing?
Thy pardon my sweet saint I implore,
My soul ne're disconform'd from thine before.

Nor will I now: My tears shall flow
No more, I will be blest 'cause thou art so.
I'll borrow comfort from thy happy state,
In bliss I'll sympathize with thee
As once I did in misery,
And by reflection will be fortunate.
I'll practice now, what's done above,
And by thy happy state my own improve.

THE RESIGNATION

Long have I view'd, long have I thought,
And held with trembling hand this bitter draught,
'Twas now just to my lips applied,
Nature shrank in, and all my courage dy'd.
But now resolv'd, and firm I'll be,
Since Lord, 'tis mingled, and reach'd out by Thee.

I'll trust my great Physician's skill,
I know what he prescribes can ne'er be ill;
To each disease He knows what's fit,
I own Him wise and good, and do submit.
I'll now no longer grieve or pine,
Since 'tis Thy pleasure Lord, it shall be mine.

Thy med'cine puts me to great smart,
Thou'st wounded me in my most tender part;
But 'tis with a design to cure,
I must and will Thy sovereign touch endure.
All that I priz'd below is gone,
But yet I still will pray, "Thy will be done".

Since 'tis Thy sentence I should part
With the most precious treasure of my heart,
I freely that and more resign,
My heart it self, as its delight is Thine,
My little all I give to Thee,
Thou gav'st a greater cost, Thy Son, to me.

He left true bliss and joy above,
Himself He emptied of all good, but love:
For me He freely did forsake
More good, than He from me can ever take.
A mortal life for a divine
He took, and did at last even that resign.

Take all great God, I will not grieve,
But still will wish, that I had still to give.
I hear thy voice, Thou bid'st me quit
My paradice, I bless and do submit.
I will not murmur at Thy word,
Nor beg Thy angel to sheath up his sword.

TO MY GUARDIAN ANGEL

I own – my gentle guide – that much I owe
For all thy tutelary[1] care and love,
Through life's wild maze thou'st led me hitherto,
Nor ever wilt – I hope – thy tent remove;
But yet t' have been compleatly true,
Thou should'st have guarded her life too.
Thou know'st my soul did most inhabit there,
I could have sparèd thee, t' have guarded her.

But since by thy neglect, or Heaven's decree,
She's gone t' encrease the pleasures of the blest,
Since in this sphere my sun I ne're shall see,
Grant me – kind spirit – grant me this request.

[1] = protective

When I shall ease my charge and dye,
– For sure I think thou wilt be by –
Lead me through all the numerous host above,
And bring my new-flown soul to her I love.

With what high passion shall we then embrace!
What pleasure will she make t' impart to me
The rites and methods of that sacred place,
And what a Heaven 'twill be to learn from thee!
That pleasure I shall then I fear
As ill as now my sorrow bear;
And could then any chance my life destroy,
I should I fear then dye again with joy.

THE DEFIANCE

Well Fortune, now if e're you have shewn
What you had in your power to do,
My wandring love at length had fix'd on one,
One who might please even unconstant you.
Me of this one you have deprived
On whom I stay'd my soul, in whom I liv'd,
You've shewn your power and I resign,
But now I'll shew thee Fortune, what's in mine.

I will not, no I will not grieve,
My tears within their banks shall stand;
Do what thou wilt, I am resolved to live,

Since thee I can't, I will my self command.
I will my passions so controul
That neither they, nor thou shalt hurt my soul;
I'll run so counter to thy will,
Thy good I'll relish, but not feel thy ill.

I felt the shaft that last was sent,
But now thy quiver I defy.
I fear no pain from thee or discontent,
Clad in the armour of philosophy.
Thy last seiz'd on me out of guard,
Unarm'd, too far within thy reach I dar'd,
But now the field I'll dearly sell,
I'm now – at least by thee – impassable.

My soul now soars high and sublime
Beyond the spring of thy best bow,
Like those who so long on high mountains climb
Till they see rain and thunder here below.
In vain thou'lt spend thy darts on me,
My fort's too strong for thy artillery,
Thy closest aim won't touch my mind,
Here's all thy gain, still to be thought more blind.

SUPERSTITION

I care not tho it be
By the preciser sort thought Popery;
We poets can a license shew
For every thing we do,
Hear then my little saint, I'll pray to thee.

If now thy happy mind
Amidst its various joys can leasure find
T' attend to anything so low
As what I say or do,
Regard, and be what thou wast ever, kind.

Let not the blest above
Engross thee quite, but sometimes hither rove;
Fain would I thy sweet image see
And sit and talk with thee,
Nor is it curiosity but love.

Ah what delight 'twou'd be
Would'st thou sometimes by stealth converse with me!
How should I thy sweet commerce prize
And other joys despise!
Come then, I ne're was yet deny'd by thee.

I would not long detain
Thy soul from bliss, nor keep thee here in pain.
Nor should thy fellow-saints e're know
Of thy escape below,
Before thou'rt miss'd thou should'st return again.

Sure Heaven must needs thy love
As well as other qualities improve.
Come then and recreate my sight
With rays of thy pure light,
'Twill chear my eyes more than the lamps above.

But if fate's so severe,
As to confine thee to thy blissful sphere,
– And by thy absence I shall know
Whether thy state be so –
Live happy, but be mindful of me there.

THE COMPLAINT OF ADAM TURN'D OUT OF PARADISE

And must I go, and must I be no more
The tenant of this happy ground?
Can no reserves of pity me restore,
Can no atonement for my stay compound?
All the rich odours that here grow I'd give
To Heaven in incense, might I here but live.
Or if it be a grace too high
To live in Eden, let me there but dye.

Fair place, thy sweets I just began to know,
And must I leave thee now again?
Ah why does Heaven such short–liv'd bliss bestow?
A taste of pleasure, but full draught of pain.
I ask not to be chief in this blest state,
Let Heaven some other for that place create.
So 'tis in Eden, let me but have
An under–gardiner's place, 'tis all I crave.

But 'twill not do I see, I must away.
My feet prophane this sacred ground;
Stay then bright minister, one minute stay,
Let me in Eden take one farewell round.
Let me go gather but one fragrant bough
Which as a relique, I may keep and shew;
Fear not the tree of life; it were
A curse to be immortal, and not here.

Tis done; now farewel thou most happy place,
Farewel ye streams that softly creep,
I ne're again in you shall view my face.
Farewel ye bowers, in you I ne're shall sleep,
Farewel ye trees, ye flowery beds farewel,
You ne're will bless my state, nor you my smell.
Farewel thou guardian divine,
To thee my happy rival I resign.

O whither now, whither shall I repair
Exil'd from this angelic coast?
There's nothing left that's pleasant, good or fair,
The world can't recompence for Eden lost.
'Tis true, I've here a universal sway,
The creatures me as their chief lord obey;
Yet the world tho all my seat,
Can't make me happy, tho it make me great.

Had I lost lesser and but seeming bliss,
Reason my sorrows might relieve.
But when the loss great and substantial is,
To think is but to see good cause to grieve.

'Tis well I'm mortal, 'tis well I shortly must
Lose all the thoughts of Eden in the dust.
Senseless and thoughtless now I'd be,
I'd lose even my self, since I've lost Thee.

TO SLEEP

Break off thy slumber gentle god
And hither bring thy charming rod;
The rod that weeping eyes does close
And gives to melancholy hearts repose;
With that my temples stroke, and let me be
Held by thy soft captivity.
But do not all my senses bind,
Nor fetter up too close my mind:
Let mimic Fancy wake, and freely rove,
And bring th' idea of the saint I love.

Her lovely image has been brought
So often to my waking thought,
That 'tis at length worn out and dead,
And with its fair original is fled.
Or else my working over–thoughtful mind
With much attention is made blind,
Like those who look on objects bright
So long till they quite lose their sight.
Ah cruel Fates, is't not enough for you
To take my saint, but I must lose her image too?

Thee gentle charmer I implore
This my lost treasure to restore;
Thy magic vertues all apply,
Set up again my bankrupt memory.
Search every cell and corner of my brain,
And bring my fugitive again.
To thy dark cave thy self betake
And 'mong the dreams enquiry make;
Summon the best ideas to appear
And bring that form which most resembles her.

But if in all thy store there be
None – as I fear – so fair as she,
Then let thy painter Fancy, limn
Her form anew, and send it by a Dream.
Thou can'st him all her lively features tell
For sure I think thou knew'st her well.
But if description wont suffice
For him to draw a piece so nice,
Then let him to my breast and heart repair,
For sure her image is not worn out there.

THE GRANT

'Twas when the tide of the returning day
Began to chase ill forms away,
When pious dreams the sense employ,
And all within is innocence and joy,
My melancholy, thoughtful mind

O'recome, at length to sleep resign'd;
Not common sleep, for I was blest
With something more divine, more sweet than rest.

She who her fine-wrought clay had lately left,
Of whose sweet form I was bereft,
Was by kind Fancy to me brought,
And made the object of my happy thought.
Clad she was all in virgin white.
And shone with empyreal light;
A radiant glory crown'd her head,
She stream'd with light and love, and thus she said.

And why this grief and passion for the blest?
Let all your sorrows with me rest.
My state is bliss, but I should live
Yet much more happy, would you cease to grieve.
Dry up your tears - dear friend - and be
Happy in my felicity.
By this your wisdom you'll approve,
Nay - what you'd most of all commend - your love.

She spake, dissolv'd I lay and overcome,
And was with exstasie struck dumb;
But ah the fierce tumultuous joy
Its own weak being, hasten'd to destroy.
To see that lovely form appear
My spirits in such commotion were,
Sleep could no more their force controul,
They shook their fetters off, and free'd my unwilling soul.

What bliss do we oft to delusion owe!
Who would not still be cheated so!
Opinion's an ingredient
That goes so far to make up true content,
That even a dream of happiness
With real joy the soul does bless;
Let me but always dream of this,
And I will envy none their waking bliss.

THE ASPIRATION

How long great God, how long must I
Immur'd in this dark prison lye!
Where at the grates and avenues of sense
My soul must watch to have intelligence.
Where but faint gleams of thee salute my sight.
Like doubtful moon-shine in a cloudy night.
When shall I leave this magic sphere,
And be all mind, all eye, all ear!

How cold this clime! and yet my sense
Perceives even here thy influence.
Even here thy strong magnetic charms I feel,
And pant and tremble like the amorous steel.
To lower good, and beauties less divine
Sometimes my erroneous needle does decline;
But yet – so strong the sympathy –
It turns, and points again to thee.

I long to see this excellence
Which at such distance strikes my sense.
My impatient soul struggles to disengage
Her wings from the confinement of her cage.
Would'st thou great Love this prisoner once set free,
How would she hasten to be link'd with Thee.
She'd for no angel's conduct stay,
But fly, and love on all the way.

THE DEFENCE

That I am colder in my friendship grown,
My faith and constancy you blame,
But sure th' inconstancy is all your own,
I am, but you are not the same.
The flame of love must needs expire
If you subtract what should maintain the fire.

While to the laws of Vertue you were true,
You had, and might retain my heart;
Now give me leave to turn apostate too,
Since you do from your self depart.
Thus the reform'd are counted free
From schism, tho they desert the Roman See.

The strictest union to be found below
Is that which soul and body ties,
They all the mysteries of friendship know,

And with each other sympathise.
And yet the soul will bid adieu
T' her much distemper'd mate, as I leave you.

RETRACTATION

I 've often charg'd all sublunary bliss,
With vanity and emptiness:
You woods and streams have heard me oft complain
How all things, how even your delights were vain.
Methought I could with one short simple view
Glance o're all humane joys and see them through.
But now great Preacher pardon me,
I cannot wholly to thy charge agree,
For Musick sure and Friendship have no vanity.

No, each of these is a firm massy joy,
Which tho eternal, will not cloy.
Here may the venturous soul live on, and find,
Grasp what she can, that more remains behind.
Such depths of joy these living springs contain,
As man t' Eternity can never drain.
These sweets the truth of Heaven prove,
Only there's greater bliss with saints above,
Because they've better musick there, and firmer love.

THE PROSPECT

What a strange moment will that be,
My soul, how full of curiosity,
When wing'd, and ready for thy eternal flight
On th' utmost edges of thy tottering clay,
Hovering and wishing longer stay,
Thou shalt advance, and have Eternity in sight!
When just about to try that unknown sea,
What a strange moment will that be!

But yet how much more strange that state
When loosen'd from th' embrace of this close mate
Thou shalt at once be plung'd in liberty,
And move as free and active as a ray
Shot from the lucid spring of day!
Thou who just now was clogg'd with dull mortality,
How wilt thou bear the mighty change, how know
Whether thou'rt then the same or no!

Then to strange mansions of the air
And stranger company must thou repair!
What a new scene of things will then appear!
The world thou by degrees wast taught to know
Which lessen'd thy surprise below,
But knowledge all at once will overflow thee there.
That world as the first man did this, thou'lt see,
Ripe-grown, in full maturity.

There with bright splendours must thou dwell,
And be what – only those pure forms can tell.
There must thou live a while, gaze and admire,
Till the great angel's trump this fabrick shake,
And all the slumbring dead awake,
Then to thy old, forgotten state thou must retire.
This union then will seem as strange, or more,
Than thy new liberty before.

Now for the greatest change prepare,
To see the only great, the only fair.
Vail now thy feeble eyes, gaze and be blest;
Here all thy turns and revolutions cease,
Here's all serenity and peace:
Thou'rt to the centre come, the native seat of rest.
There's now no further change nor need there be;
When one shall be variety.

THE RETURN

Dear contemplation, my divinest joy,
When I thy sacred mount ascend
What heavenly sweets my soul employ!
Why can't I there my days for ever spend?
When I have conquer'd thy steep heights with pain
What pity 'tis that I must down again!

And yet I must; my passions would rebel
Should I too long continue here:
No, here I must not think to dwell,
But mind the duties of my proper sphere.
So angels, tho they heaven's glories know,
Forget not to attend their charge below.

THE 137th PSALM PARAPHRASED TO THE 7th VERSE

Beneath a reverend gloomy shade,
Where Tigris and Euphrates cut their way,
With folded arms and heads supinely laid
We sate, and wept out all the tedious day,
Within its banks grief could not be
Contain'd, when Sion, we remember'd thee.

Our harps with which we oft have sung
In solemn strains the great Jehovah's praise,
Our warbling harps upon the trees we hung,
Too deep our grief to hear their pleasing lays.
Our harps were sad, as well as we,
And tho by angels touch'd, would yield no harmony.

But they who forc'd us from our seat,
The happy Land, and sweet abode of rest,
Had one way left to be more cruel yet,
And ask'd a song from hearts with grief opprest.

Let's hear, say they, upon the lyre
One of the anthems of your Hebrew quire.

How can we frame our voice to sing
The hymns of joy, festivity, and praise,
To those who're aliens to our heavenly King,
And want a taste for such exalted layes?
Our harps will here refuse to sound;
An holy song is due to holy ground.

No, dearest Sion, if we can
So far forget thy melancholy state
As now thou mourn'st, to sing one chearful strain,
This ill be added to our ebb of fate;
Let neither harp nor voice e're try
One hallelujah more, but ever silent lye.

THE 139th PSALM PARAPHRASED TO THE 14th VERSE

In vain, great God, in vain I try
T' escape Thy quick all–seaching eye.
Thou with one undivided view
Dost look the whole creation through.
The unshap'd embryo's of my mind
Not yet to form or likeness wrought,
The tender rudiments of thought
Thou see'st, before she can her own conception find.

My private walks to thee are known,
In solitude I'm not alone;
Thou round my bed a guard dost keep,
Thy eyes are open, while mine sleep.
My softest whispers reach Thy ear:
'Tis vain to fancy secrecy;
Which way so e're I turn Thou'rt there,
I am all round beset with Thy immensity.

I can't wade through this depth, I find,
It drowns and swallows up my mind.
'Tis like Thy immense Deity.
I cannot fathom that, or Thee.
Where then shall I a refuge find
From Thy bright comprehensive eye?
Whither, O whither shall I fly,
What place is not possest by Thy all-filling mind!

If to the heavenly orbs I fly,
There is Thy seat of majesty.
If down to Hell's abyss I go
There I am sure to meet Thee too.
Should I with the swift wings of Light
Seek some remote and unknown Land,
Thou soon would'st overtake my flight,
And all my motions rule with Thy long-reaching hand.

Should I t' avoid Thy piercing sight,
Retire behind the skreen of Night,
Thou canst with one celestial ray
Dispel the shades, and make it day.

Nor need'st Thou by such mediums see;
The force of Thy clear radiant sight,
Depends not on our grosser light;
On light Thou sitt'st enthron'd, 'tis ever day with Thee.

The springs which life and motion give
Are Thine, by Thee I move and live.
My frame has nothing hid from Thee,
Thou know'st my whole anatomy.
T' an hymn of praise I'le tune my lyre;
How amazing is this work of Thine!
With dread I into my self retire,
For tho the metal's base, the stamp is all divine.

TO DR. PLOT, ON HIS NATURAL HISTORY OF STAFFORDSHIRE[1]

What strange perversity is this of man!
When 'twas a crime to taste th' inlightning tree
He could not then his hand refrain,
None then so inquisitive, so curious as he.
But now he has liberty to try and know
God's whole plantation below;
Now the angelic fruit may be
Tasted by all whose arms can reach the tree:
H' is now by licence careless made,
The tree neglects to climb, and sleeps beneath the shade.

[1] Robert Plot, LLD., a celebrated antiquary, born 1641, died April 30th, 1696. His 'Natural History' *supra* was published in 1686.

Such drowsie sedentary souls have they
Who could patriarchal years live on,
Fixed to hereditary clay,
And know no climate but their own.
Contracted to their narrow sphere,
Rest before knowledge they prefer,
And of this globe wherein they dwell
No more than of the heavenly orbs can tell.
As if by Nature plac'd below
Not on this earth to dwell, but to take root and grow.

Dull souls, why did great Nature take such care
To write in such a splendid character;
If man the only thing below
That can pretend her hand to know,
Her fair–writ volume does despise,
And tho design'd for wisdom won't be wise?
Th' Almighty gets no praise from this dull kind,
The sun was never worship'd by the blind.
Such ignorance can ne're devotion raise,
They will want wisdom and their Maker praise.

They only can this tribute duely yield
Whose active spirits range abroad,
Who traverse o're all Nature's field
And view the great magnificence of God.
They see the hidden wealth of Nature's store
Fall down and learnedly adore;
But they most justly yet this tribute pay
Who don't contemplate only, but display,
Comment on Nature's text, and to the sense

Expose her latent excellence;
Who like the sun, not only travel o're
The world, but give it light that others may adore.

In th' head of these heroic few
Our learnèd author here appears in view,
Whose searching genius like lamp of day
Does the Earth's furniture display,
Nor suffers to lye bury'd and unknown
Nature's rich talent or his own.
Drake and Columbus do in thee revive,
And we from thy research as much receive.
Thou art as great as they, for 'tis all one
New worlds to find, or nicely to describe the known.

On mighty hero, our whole isle survey,
Advance thy standard, conquer all the way.
Let nothing but the sea controul
The progress of thy active soul.
Act like a pious courteous ghost,
And to mankind retrieve what's lost.
With thy victorious charitable hand
Point out the hidden treasures of our Land.
Envy or Ignorance do what they will,
Thou hast a blessing from the Muses' hill.
Great be thy spirit as thy works divine,
Show thou thy Maker's praise, we poets will sing thine.

THE EXCHANGE

When Corydon had lost his liberty
And felt the tyrant's heavy chain;
He swore, could he but once get free,
He'd never, no, he'd never love again.

But stay dull shepherd, if you quench your fire,
Too dear will you buy your liberty:
Let not such vigorous heats expire,
I'll teach thee how to love, and yet be free.

Take bright Urania[1] to thy amorous breast.
To her thy flaming heart resign;
Void not the room, but change the guest,
And let thy sensual love commence divine.

The swain obey'd, and when he once had known
This foretaste of the joys above,
He vow'd, though he might be his own,
Yet he would ever, yes he'd ever love.

THE REFINEMENT

Well 'twas a hard decree of Fate,
My soul, to clip thy pinions so,
To make thee leave thy pure ethereal state,
And breath the vapours of this stream below,

[1] = the muse of astronomy

Where he that can pretend to have
Most freedom, 's still his body's slave.

Was e're a substance so divine
With such an unlike consort joyn'd?
Did ever things so wide, so close combine
As massy clods and sun–beams, earth and mind?
When yet two souls can ne're agree
In friendship, but by parity.

Unequal match! what wilt thou do,
My soul, to raise thy plumes again?
How wilt thou this gross vehicle subdue,
And thy first bliss, first purity obtain?
Thy consort how wilt thou refine,
And be again all o're divine?

Fix on the sovereign thy fair eye,
And kindle in thy breast a flame;
Wind up thy passions to a pitch so high
Till they melt down, and rarify thy frame.
Like the great prophet then aspire,
Thy chariot will like his, be fire.[1]

TO MELANCHOLY

Mysterious passion, dearest pain,
Tell me, what wondrous charms are these,
With which thou dost torment or please,
I grieve to be thy slave, yet would not freedom gain.

[1] = 2 Kings 2:11

No tyranny like thine we know,
That half so cruel e're appear'd,
And yet thou'rt lov'd as well as fear'd,
Perhaps the only tyrant that is so.

Long have I been thy votary,
Thou'st led me out to woods and groves,
Made'st me despise all other loves,
And give up all my passions, all my soul to thee.
Thee for my first companion did I chuse,
First, even before my darling Muse;
And yet I know of thee no more
Than those who never did thy shrine adore.

Thou'rt mystery and riddle all,
Like those thou inspirest, thou lov'st to be
In darkness and obscurity.
Even learnèd Athens thee an unknown God might call.[1]
Strange contraries in thee combine,
Both Hell and Heaven in thee meet,
Thou greatest bitter, greatest sweet,
No pain is like thy pain, no pleasure too like thine.

'Tis the grave doctrin of the Schools
That contraries can never be
Consistent in th' high'st degree,
But thou must stand exempt from these dull narrow rules.
And yet 'tis said the brightest mind
Is that which is by thee refin'd.
See here a greater mystery,
Thou mak'st us wise, yet ruin'st our philosophy.

[1] = Acts 17:23

THE DISCONTENT

Not that it is not my fate,
to stand upon the dangerous heights of State,
Nor that I cannot be possest
Of th' hidden treasures of the East,
Nor that I cannot bathe in Pleasure's spring,
And rifle all the sweets which Nature's gardens bring
Do I repine, my destiny,
I can all these despise, as well as you deny.

It shall not discompose my mind
Though not one star above to me prove kind.
Their influence may sway the sea,
But make not the least change in me.
They neither can affect my state, nor bless,
Their greatest gifts are small, and my desires are less.
My vessel bears but little sail,
What need I then a full and swelling gale?

And yet I'm discontented too,
Perhaps y' aspiring souls as much as you;
We both in equal trouble live,
But for much different causes grieve,
You, that these guilded joys you can't obtain;
And I, because I know they're empty all and vain.
You still pursue in hopes to find,
I stand and dare not flatter on my mind.

This tree of knowledge is, I see,
Still fatal to poor man's felicity.
That which yields others great repast,
Can't please my now enlighten'd taste.
Before, tho I could nothing solid find,
Yet still with specious prospects I could please my mind.
Now all the farthest I can see
Is one perpetual round of vanity.

BEAUTY

Best object of the passion most divine,
What excellence can Nature shew
In all her various stores below,
Whose charms may be compar'd to thine?
Even light it self is therefore fair
Only because it makes thy sweets appear.

Thou streaming splendour of the Face divine
What in the regions above,
Do saints like thee adore or love,
What excellence is there like thine?
I except not the Divinity,
That great and sovereign good, for thou art He.

He's Beautie's vast abyss and boundless sea,
The primitive and greatest Fair;
All His perfections beauties are,
Beauty is all the Deity.

Some streams from this vast ocean flow,
And that is all that pleases, all that's fair below.

Divine perfection who alone art all
That various scene of excellence
Which pleases either man or sense,
Tho thee by different names we call!
Search Nature through, thou still wilt be
The sum of all that's good in her variety.

Love, that most active passion of the mind,
Whose roving flame does traverse o're
All Nature's good, and reach for more,
Still to thy magic sphere's confin'd.
'Tis beauty all we can desire,
Beauty's the native mansion of Love's fire.

Those finer spirits who from the croud retire
To study Nature's artful scheme,
Or speculate a theorem,
What is't but beauty they admire?
And they too who enamour'd are
Of Virtue's face, love her because she's fair.

No empire, sovereign Beauty, is like thine,
Thou reign'st unrivall'd and alone,
And universal is thy throne,
Stoicks themselves to thee resign.
From passions be they ne'er so free
Something they needs must love, and that is thee.

He whom we all adore, that mighty He,
Owns thy supream dominion,
And happy lives in thee alone,
We'er blest in Him, and He in thee:
In thee He's infinitely blest,
Thou art the inmost center of His rest.

Pleas'd with thy form which in His essence shin'd,
Th' Almighty chose to multiply
This flower of His Divinity
And lesser beauties soon design'd.
The unform'd chaos He remov'd,
Tinctur'd the mass with thee, and then it lov'd.

But do not thou my soul, fixt here remain,
All streams of beauty here below
Do from that immense ocean flow,
And thither they should lead again.
Trace then these streams, till thou shalt be
At length o'rewhelm'd in Beauty's boundless sea.

LOVE

Imperial passion! Sacred fire!
When we of meaner subjects sing,
Thou tun'st our harps, thou dost our souls inspire,
'Tis love directs the quill, 'tis love strikes every string.
But where's another Deity
T' inspire the man that sings of thee?

W' are by mistaken chymists told,
That the most active part of all
The various compound cast in Nature's mould,
Is that which they mercurial spirit call.
But sure 'tis love they should have said,
Without this even their spirit is dead.

Love's the great spring of Nature's wheel,
Love does the mass pervade and move,
What 'scapes the sun's, does thy warm influence feel,
The Universe is kept in tune by love.
Thou Nature giv'st her sympathy,
The center has its charm from thee.

Love did great Nothing's barren womb
Impregnate with his genial fire;
From this first parent did all creatures come,
Th' Almighty will'd, and made all by desire.
Nay more, among the sacred Three,
The third subsistence is from thee.

The happiest order of the blest
Are those whose tide of love's most high,
The bright seraphick host, who're more possest
Of good, because more like the Deity.
T' him they advance as they improve
Their noble heat, for God is love.

Shall then a passion so divine
Stoop down and mortal beauties know?
Nature's great statute law did ne're design
That heavenly fire should kindle here below;
Let it ascend and dwell above,
The proper element of love.

THE CONSUMMATION: A PINDARIQUE ODE

The rise of monarchies, and their long, weighty fall
My Muse out–soars; she proudly leaves behind
The pomps of Courts, she leaves our little all,
To be the humble song of a less reaching mind.
In vain I curb her tow'ring flight;
All I can here present's too small.
She presses on, and now has lost their sight,
She flyes, and hastens to relate
The last and dreadful scene of Fate,
Nature's great solemn funeral.
I see the mighty angel stand
Cloath'd with a cloud, and rain–bow round his head,
His right foot on the sea, his other on the land,
He lifted up his dreadful arm, and thus he said;
By the mysterious great Three–One
Whose power we fear, and truth adore
I swear the fatal thred is spun,
Nature shall breath her last, and Time shall be no more.
The antient stager of the day
Has run his minutes out, and numb'rd all his way.
The parting isthmus is thrown down

And all shall now be overflown.
Time shall no more her under–current know
But one with great Eternity shall grow,
Their streams shall mix, and in one circling channel flow.
He spake, Fate writ the sentence with her iron pen,
And mighty thundrings said, Amen!
What dreadful sound's this strikes my ear?
'Tis sure th' archangels trump I hear,
Nature's great passing bell, the only call
Of God's that will be heard by all.
The Universe takes the alarm, the sea
Trembles at the great angel's sound,
And roars almost as loud as he,
Seeks a new channel, and would fain run under ground.
The Earth it self does no less quake,
And all throughout, down to the center shake,
The graves unclose, and the deep sleepers there awake.
The sun arrested in his way,
He dares not forward go,
But wondring stands at the great hurry here below;
The stars forget their laws, and like loose planets stray.
See how the elements resign
Their numerous charge, the scatter'd atoms home repair,
Some from the Earth, some from the sea, some from the air:
They know the great alarm,
And in confus'd mixt numbers swarm,
Till rang'd and sever'd by the chymistry divine.
The Father of mankind amaz'd to see
The globe too narrow for his progeny.
But 'tis the closing of the age,
And all the actors now at once must grace the stage.

Now Muse exalt thy wing, be bold and dare,
Fate does a wondrous scene prepare;
The central fire which hitherto did burn
Dull like a lamp in a most clammy urn,
Fann'd by the breath divine begins to glow,
The fiends are all amaz'd below.
But that will no confinement know,
Breaks through its sacred fence, and plays more free
Than thou with all thy vast Pindaric liberty.

Nature does sick of a strong fever lye:
The fire the subterraneous vaults does spoil;
The mountains sweat, the sun does boil;
The sea, her mighty pulse, beats high;
The waves of fire more proudly rowl;
The fiends in their deep caverns howl,
And with the frightful trumpet mix their hideous cry.
Now is the tragic scene begun;
The fire in triumph marches on;
The Earth's girt round with flames, and seems another sun.

But whither does this lawless judgement roam?
Must all promiscuously expire
A sacrifice in Sodom's fire?
Read thy commission, Fate; sure all are not thy due,
No, thou must save the virtuous few
But where's the angel guardian to avert the doom?

Lo, with a mighty host he's come:
I see the parted clouds give way;
I see the banner of the cross display.

Deaths' conqueror in pomp appears,
In His right hand a palm He bears,
And in His looks redemption wears:
Th' illustrious glory of this scene
Does the dispairing saints inspire
With joy, with rapture, and desire;
Kindles the brighter life that dormant lay within,
Th' awaken'd virtue does its strength display
Melts and refines their drossy clay;
New–cast into a pure ætherial frame,
They fly and mount aloft in vehicles of flame.
Slack here my Muse thy roving wing,
And now the world's untun'd, let down thy high–set string.

FREEDOM

I do not ask thee Fate, to give
This little span a long reprieve.
The pleasures here are all so poor and vain,
I care not hence how soon I'm gone.
Date as thou wilt my time, I shan't complain;
May I but still live free, and call it all my own.

Let my sand slide away apace;
I care not, so I hold the glass,
Let me my time, my books, my self enjoy,
Give me from cares a sure retreat;
Let no impertinence my hours imploy,
That's in one word, kind Heaven, let me ne'er be great.

In vain from chains and fetters free
The great man boasts of liberty.
He's pinnion'd up by formal rules of State;
Can ne'er from noise and dust retire;
He's haunted still by crouds that round him wait,
His lot's to be in pain, as that of fools t' admire.

Mean while the swain has calm repose,
Freely he comes and freely goes.
Thus the bright stars whose station is most high,
Are fix'd, and by strict measures move,
While lower planets wanton in the sky,
Are bound to no set laws, but humoursomly rove.

TO HIS MUSE

Come Muse, let's cast up our accounts, and see
How much you are in debt to me:
You've reign'd thus long the mistress of my heart,
You've been the ruling planet of my days,
In my spare-hours you've had your part,
Ev'n now my servile mind your sovereign will obeys.
Too great such service to be free,
Tell me what I'm to have for being thy votary?

You have preferments in your gift, you say,
You can with gold my service pay;
I fear thy boast, your sacred hill I'm told

In a poor, curs'd and barren country lies;
Besides what's state to me, or gold,
These you long since have taught me to despise.
To put me off with this, would be
Not to reward, but tax my ill proficiency.

But fame you say will make amends for all,
This you your sovereign blessing call,
The only lasting good that never dies,
A good which never can be bought too dear,
Which all the wise and virtuous prize,
The gods too with delight their praises hear.
This shall my portion be, you say,
You'll crown my head with an immortal bay.[1]

Give me a place less high, and more secure,
This dangerous good I can't endure.
The peaceful banks which profound silence keep
The little boat securely passes by,
But where with noise the waters creep
Turn off with care, for treacherous rocks are nigh.
Then Muse farewell, I see your store
Can't pay for what is past, and I can trust no more.

[1] = the bay wreath, *Laurus Nobilis*, placed around the head of a poet or conqueror

A memorial plaque can be seen on the North wall of St. Andrews Church, Bemerton:

H S E
JOHANNES NORRIS
Parochiae hujus Rector
Ubi annos 20 bene Latuit
Curae Pastorali et Literis vacans:
Quo in Recefsu Sibi posuit
Late jam p. Orbem sparsa
Ingenij paris ac Pietatis
Monumenta

Obijt Ano Dni 1711
AEtais 54

Translation of the above:

JOHN NORRIS
Rector of this parish
Where for 20 years he lived a good life in retirement,
using his leisure for pastoral care and literature.
In this retreat he set up for himself monuments of
equal genius and piety, now widely scattered
through the world.

He died in the year of our Lord 1711, aged 54.